JAZZ PEOPLE

by VALERIE WILMER

with photographs by the author

A DA CAPO PAPERBACK

Library of Congress Cataloging in Publication Data

Wilmer, Valerie.
  Jazz people.
  (A Da Capo Paperback)
  Reprint. Originally published: 3rd. ed. London: Allison &
Busby, 1977.
  Includes index.
  1. Jazz music—Addresses, essays, lectures. 2. Jazz musicians—
United States—Biography. I. Title. II. Series.
ML3507.W55   1990   785.42′092′2 [B]   85-5270
ISBN 0-306-80434-4

This Da Capo Press paperback edition of Valerie Wilmer's *Jazz People* is an
unabridged republication of the third edition published in London in 1977.
It is reprinted by arrangement with the author.

Published by Da Capo Press, Inc.
A Subsidiary of Plenum Publishing Corporation
233 Spring Street, New York, N.Y. 10013

To Herbie Lovelle and
Edgar and Barbara Blakeney

A combination of Stateside *bonhomie* and Lancashire
hospitality that turned me on to the scene when
the music had already turned me around.

Contents

Author's Note

I owe more than thanks to the following helpful people; they'll know why: Edward and Fran Blackwell, Edgar and Barbara Blakeney, Harry Carney, Buck Clayton, Peter Clayton, Bill and Lily Coleman, Henry Coker, Don DeMicheal, Art Farmer, Benny and Bobbie Golson, Babs Gonzales, Paul Jeffrey, Herb Lovelle, Dan Morgenstern, Howard and Sandy McGhee, Gene Ramey, Buddy Tate, Earle Warren, Dicky Wells; and also to the late Red Allen, the late Joe Gordon and the late Rex Stewart.

Acknowledgements are due to the following publications, in which versions of some of these interviews first appeared: *Down Beat, Jazz Monthly, King, Melody Maker, Soul Illustrated.*

V.W.

Preface to Third Edition

Looking back at my Introduction eight years after it was written I see that I feel pretty much the same about the way in which the exponents of so-called "jazz" are forced to earn a living.

The personal lives of these fourteen individuals have changed – mostly, it should be said, for the better, but the situation for the Black artist who is unable or unwilling to compromise is still inequitable. And for the majority of white players who have chosen to create within this essentially African-American form, the situation is depressingly similar.

Although the past decade has seen academic opportunities opening up for musicians and grants being made available from different foundations, the state of the economy is such that it has actually become harder for the creative player to remain faithful to his or her art. For all these reasons I stand by most of what I wrote in 1969.

Valerie Wilmer. London, 1977

In the beginning there was Herbie
. . . and Earle and Gene and Dicky and Buck

The first jazz musician I ever interviewed was almost, if not quite, as conventional as the hypothetical man-next-door. His dress was sober, his speech unremarkable and his manner was friendly. As far as I could make out at the time, he didn't get drunk every night, stick a needle in his arm or beat his wife. In fact, the most unconventional thing about him was a pair of outrageous floral underpants which he immodestly displayed as he dashed from bedroom to bathroom and back again. As he hurriedly changed into his stage suit, he continued to carry on a remarkable, disjointed conversation with the assembled company while firing off inconsequential career details for the benefit of a nervous eighteen-year-old. Me.

I carelessly betrayed my teenage naïvety as I fumbled with pen and notebook and told him that I wanted to write a book about jazz one day. Herbie Lovelle glanced in the mirror and adjusted his bow-tie, then picked up his drumsticks. He gave me an appraising look and suggested blandly: " Why don't you start now? "

In a sense I did just that. It's taken me years to discover the way to the musician's heart and has included a generous share of hangovers and hangups along the way, but during that time I've learnt more about the music from the jazz people them-selves than any number of concerts could teach. Some gave me the runaround before I ran them to earth, but the majority have given willingly of their time. A few of the most interesting have helped me write this book.

A common expression in the jazz argot is " to pay one's dues ", and that is more or less what this compilation of fact and opinion is about. The phrase originates from the actual monthly dues paid to the union, but it is a universally accepted comment on the hazards of the day-to-day jazz existence. To have paid one's dues is considered a prerequisite to musical and personal maturity. It crops up frequently here as fourteen outstanding and original musicians discuss their own particular problems and solutions, and it is no coincidence that these setbacks often have economic foundations.

Naturally, all artists have their cross to bear. Certainly there is no reason why opera singers, painters and dancers should be exempt from their respective frustrations, but the members of such professions tend to come from widely differing backgrounds and are mostly white, whereas the jazz people are all children of the ghetto, even if only figuratively speaking. Where they are concerned, frustration's face always bears the same bleak expression. The black existence is more than filled with the raw material that has inspired the most vital and heart-rendingly emotional of all the arts; it is choked up with it.

Because of the underprivileged environment in which they exist, the jazz people tend to be socially aware even if they have no social conscience as such. They recognise the adversities that have shaped their lives and, because they are possibly the most readily approachable of all artists, you rapidly learn from associating with them about the outside factors that have twisted the course of their seething, uninhibited music. It's something you could never learn about from listening to the records.

When this book was in progress I showed it to Eddie " Lockjaw " Davis, who is a cynical worthy at the best of times. His reaction was immediate. " Why do you want to put drugs in there? " he asked. He went on to point out that there were more doctors than musicians who were addicted, and hadn't jazz been harmed enough already by bad publicity on the subject? The same old story, in fact, that musicians have been dishing out to the more gullible members of the press for years. There are those whose reaction will be the same as his, but anyone who has been involved with the jazz life to any extent knows only too well the destructive role narcotics have played in the story of the music. All those dull, repetitive record sessions made in a hurry when the musician needed the money to support a gnawing habit, the club or concert appearance by a fumbling artist who doesn't live up to his recorded reputation — all these events, not to mention the snuffing-out of so many half-lived lives, bear the ugly shadow of the hypodermic.

So if harping on these non-musical factors seems irrelevant — especially the stress on race that is implied throughout by every musician but seldom voiced except by Randy Weston, Archie Shepp and Cecil Taylor — they are nevertheless given prominence because they disrupt the lives of the jazz people and thus, the course of the music itself. For example, the subject under discussion may have no narcotic problem himself, but a sideman involved in his important record date may be " strung out " and have an adverse effect on arrangements or compositions in which the leader has invested time and creativity. Jazz is playing the way that you feel and you know that the leader is going to get pretty bitter at the situation in the studio. His playing will suffer, the record will be dismissed as having nothing new to add and he will not be invited to make another. A hypothetical situation, true, but there are any number of similar, real situations.

Some people have suggested that I include a couple of valiant white musicians in order to make this picture of the jazz world more comprehensive. My assembled fourteen are all black because however good, however great, however emotionally moving or aesthetically stimulating the individual white musician *can* be, his role is usually only that of an imitator. There are some white musicians who are more creative than some of their black counterparts but, generally speaking, I share an opinion expressed ·by the pianist, Randy Weston : " I don't care if Gary Burton is a good vibraharpist or Jack Teagarden did play good trombone, it's so unimportant. The fact is that the creative source of this music has always been from the black people."

The interview format has been widely used in jazz literature as a source of information on the background of the music and I have adhered to it here. I could have translated the musicians' words into my own and thus posed as the great commentator on the psychological makeup of the jazz musician and the sociological structure of the scene, but I prefer to let the musicians do the talking themselves. I never get tired of hearing them speak.

Each interview has been expanded into a kind of profile

that attempts to deal with one particular facet of the jazz life. Here and there opinions clash and, of course, what each man says is entirely subjective. However, different eras inspire and nurture differing attitudes and the twenty-five years or so that separate Buck Clayton and Joe Turner from Billy Higgins and Archie Shepp are responsible for a gulf of opinion as wide as the environmental and educational gap between Turner, an illiterate blues singer who was born in Kansas City in the Mid-West, and pianist Cecil Taylor, an academic, aesthete and graduate from the New England Conservatory of Music in Boston, Massachusetts. It is interesting, therefore, to note when and where the musicians were born.

This is especially so when one considers that a man like Buck Clayton, who was born in 1911 when jazz was hardly a decade old, has remained a truly beautiful and enduring trumpet player in spite of the rapid and radical changes that the music has undergone in his lifetime. He is one of the first gentlemen of swing and was a stalwart sideman in the classic Count Basie band from 1936–43, and his good and productive life in jazz has continued from both economic and artistic standpoints. There are few musicians from his era who make as good a living as Buck Clayton does, and even fewer who continue to think about creativity within the limitations imposed by their own tradition. Each time I have heard Buck play, however, he seems to outdo his previous performance. He is an exceptional man in many ways, not the least being his willingness to answer the most mundane questions put to him by the jazz fanatic and amateur scribe. I should know, because I was one of them when I first met him. Music is still a challenge for him and here he considers his personal fortunes.

Big Joe Turner comes from the same era as Buck — he was born in the same year, in fact — and their careers intersected in the productive milieu of the Kansas City nightclubs of the 1930s. Turner is one of the great instinctive blues singers, a man with minimal musical knowledge who sings only what his emotions suggest. His singing is direct and uncomplicated, yet sophisticated in comparison with the country blues. Turner's is the blues of the big city, outdated in style when contrasted with the soul singers popular with the black American public in the 1960s, but nevertheless enduring. He was the forerunner of the jazz singer, an influence on countless other big band shouters like Jimmy Witherspoon and B. B. King who were themselves an inspiration to some of the less gospel-orientated singers who have hollered their blues into the Top Forty.

Thelonious Monk, Clark Terry, Howard McGhee and Eddie Davis were all born between 1918 and 1921, yet their respective musical conceptions and careers have little in common. The diversity of the jazz life itself is reflected in their individual, instantly recognisable, and widely contrasting sounds. Eddie " Lockjaw " Davis is a New York-born tenor saxophonist who has led his own groups, worked with the Count Basie band as saxophonist-cum-road manager, and shared a hard-hitting two-tenor combo with the little Chicago wizard, Johnny Griffin. Davis is one of the most observant and eloquent commentators on the jazz life and apart from his productive career as an active musician, he has put in a spell behind the desk of a major New York booking agency and knows all the ins and outs of the economics of the music business. His frankness in talking about selling an art form is unusual, especially as he refuses to give jazz that status, calling it " craft ", and takes the line of attacking equally the shortcomings of musician, club owner and promoter.

Clark Terry has also worked with the Basie band, with Duke Ellington, Quincy Jones and practically every notable big band you care to name. He is a highly individual trumpeter and fluegelhorn player who is respected as much for his technique as his artistry. He is one of the few blacks who have secured steady employment in the lucrative recording studios and a staff job on a major television network, a feat which has earned him the envy of some black musicians and the disparagement of others, not to mention discrimination from the white establishment. Clark Terry has probably made more money than anyone else in this book with the exception of Monk, but he has paid some heavy dues to reach his position. Only he knows how much his soul has suffered in the quest for respectability and riches and only a man from a poverty-stricken background can understand the pleasure they give. I will never forget an incident that occurred when I stayed in

New York as the guest of tenor saxophonist and composer Benny Golson and his wife. Benny was earning around 30,000 dollars a year at the time as a busy arranger and I made the mistake of joking about his extravagance. He is one of the most polite and gentle men I have ever met and so I was hardly prepared for the way he rounded on me. " If you'd had to stick cardboard in your shoes before you went out in the snow you'd know what money means ! " he said heatedly. I never made that mistake again.

Thelonious Monk is one of the most original pianists and composers in the history of jazz. He is an innovator, one of the founding fathers of the harmonic revolution of the early 1940s that changed the course of jazz. Monk has seldom been interviewed; he prefers his music to do the talking. Yet when he does talk about his life, often laughing off serious suggestions or questions, he reveals more about himself than he realises. In conversation he is as unpredictable as his angular, fragmented music, and almost as rewarding.

Trumpeter Howard McGhee, born in 1918, is two years older than Monk and Terry. In common with other musicians of his age, his grounding was in the big swing bands, but he is best known as one of the most recorded soloists of the bebop era; only Dizzy Gillespie and the late Fats Navarro have the edge on him in technique. He is also one of the many musicians from that period who succumbed to narcotics and, unlike some of the jazz people, is prepared to discuss the subject with frankness. One of the key figures of the bop revolution, he has known what it is to make thousands of dollars in a day and end up in the gutter overnight.

No doubt narcotics have also pressurised some musician-addicts into producing more music more quickly, but the heroin addiction that caused the disappearance of so many of the jazz artists, great and small, who were active in McGhee's era and after is thankfully in decline. Nowadays it is not hip to be " strung out " although some of the young revolutionaries do have rather amusing dual-standards about some of the other drugs still commonly used by musicians. I met one famous saxophonist in New York at the time when the free musicians were just breaking through into print and were very image-conscious. He was anxious to point out the extent of his spiritual involvement and rejection of worldly values. " We're not like those oldtimey cats with all their booze and drugs," he insisted. " Tell them the musicians of today are clean. Our minds must be clear to produce beauty; we don't have any time for any of that shit." A year later this paragon turned up in London. Even before I had finished greeting him he was hustling me : " Where can I get some coke, baby? I know you can turn me on."

Vocalist and comedian Babs Gonzales grew up with bop also, although his personal contribution was negligible from a musical point of view and he would be the first to admit that he doesn't have the greatest " pipes " in the world. Babs is a year younger than Howard McGhee and has worked and recorded with Dizzy Gillespie and the late pianist and composer, Tadd Dameron. He has the distinction of being the only man in this book to have published his autobiography, and as jazz is nothing without humour, he has plenty to spare when adding another chapter.

Art Farmer, Jimmy Heath, Randy Weston and Jackie McLean (1926–28) belong to the second wave of beboppers. They are neither the innovators nor their compadres but the consolidators of existing concepts. They are original but not " originals " in the sense that Monk is, and possibly McLean alone has shaken off his earliest influences to emerge as a total, contemporary artist. Growing up in the shadow of a giant is always a handicap and it took the young saxophonist some years to escape being saddled with the label " imitator ". His involvement with Charlie Parker's concept and emergence as a personal stylist provides the topic in this chapter.

Farmer is a trumpeter turned fluegelhornist who has worked with Horace Silver, Gerry Mulligan and Lionel Hampton and co-led the Jazztet with Benny Golson. He also led his own combo for several years before moving to Vienna, and has worked extensively as a soloist in Europe as well as America. If I was asked to point out any one musician whose name was synonymous with integrity, it would be Art Farmer. He has successfully retained his identity in the heterogeneous jazz whirlpool and kept his integrity intact from musical and personal standpoints alike. He is a cool player in the age of intensity, and a strong personality in the day of the commonplace.

Tenor saxophonist and composer Jimmy Heath is usually referred to as " the brother of the bassist with the Modern Jazz Quartet " instead of being recognised as a creative musician in his own right. Ironically, he has been playing the saxophone for longer than his better-known brother, Percy, has been involved in music. Heath, like pianist Randy Weston, bears the stigma of " musicians' musician ", which means that he is never extended much recognition outside the bandroom. He is a thorough, persevering saxophonist in the hard bop style who refuses to be a copycat or ape the superficial mannerisms of contemporary jazz in order to make a successful splash. He never gets his name in the jazz polls, seldom makes a record, but his single-mindedness is far from unique.

Randy Weston is so single-minded that he has given up the American scene for dead. He dislikes the innovations that have been introduced in the last ten years by Ornette Coleman, Cecil Taylor and John Coltrane, and instead of letting his talents decay and wasting his creative mind, he has given free rein to a hidden desire and made his home in Africa. Years ago the late trumpeter Joe Gordon said to me, " America is fucked up ", and Randy shares this opinion. It is another of his reasons for heading East. In Morocco he has found the love and sense of brotherhood that seem to be missing in his homeland. He has no intention of returning to a country where the climate is hostile and unreceptive towards his essentially uncommercial music.

Randy, together with the late Elmo Hope, is one of the few pianists who adapted Monk's harmonic concept to their needs, most pianists of their generation preferring to use the more melodic approach of Bud Powell as their standard. Another pianist who used Monk's concept initially is Cecil Taylor, who was born in Long Island, New York, in 1933 and is a unique force in the avant garde both as pianist, composer and formulator of a totally new approach to American music. Taylor's originality and potency have been overlooked for years but he is at last emerging from the shadows of obscurity in terms of recognition if not financial reward. Cecil feels that as long as the jazz clubs and record companies are owned by the "white power structure", his circumstances can hardly change. His words echo what poet, playwright and jazz critic LeRoi Jones once told a white nightclub owner : " In jazz, you're the white power structure. You hire and fire, you're just a shopkeeper in a very hip ghetto situation."

Billy Higgins, born in Texas in 1936 and raised in Los Angeles, has the distinction of being not only one of the most versatile of today's jazz percussionists but one of the first of the "free" drummers who ignored the strict time-keeping that was mandatory until recently. He was an early associate of Ornette Coleman in California at the time when it was hipper to pour scorn on the saxophonist's experiments and hustle him off the bandstand. He is perceptive in thought, artistic in perpetration. He is a drummerman-for-all-seasons, whose comments here on the art of lovemaking in music inspired these words from pianist Horace Silver when they first appeared in *Down Beat* : " I meet many young drummers in my travels who ask me what they should study and who they should listen to, etc., etc. I think Billy tells them pretty much where it's at, and I recommend that all young drummers read and digest that article very carefully."

Jazz, as the music of an oppressed minority, has long provided food for white social commentators, beginning with Sidney Finkelstein's book, *Jazz — A Peoples' Music*, but rarely has it produced its own. In the tenor saxophonist, composer and playwright Archie Shepp, the music has its own advocate of its intrinsic blackness. Shepp, who was first introduced to the jazz public via his recordings with Cecil Taylor, is one of the most outspoken voices in the jazz avant garde and one of the most intellectual of musicians, too. Archie looks at jazz from a strictly black viewpoint without any of the illusions created by the critical standards of the past.

Without the cooperation of these fourteen men, some of them good friends, others merely casual acquaintances, this book would never have been. There are a number of mean and petty musicians but on the whole the jazz people are as warm and generous as their music. Occasionally I have caught myself wishing they were all as articulate as Shepp or the late

Rex Stewart, as mercilessly observant as Eddie Davis or as perceptive as Art Farmer, but as long as I am not made victim of the put-on, a technique of leg-pulling and exaggeration reserved by musicians for the benefit of the uninitiated, I have no cause for complaint.

That the jazz people have given me an occasional glimpse of more than their music is cause for a lifetime's rejoicing.

Valerie Wilmer, 1967–69

Chapter One

The Art of Perception

The player himself is the most severe critic of them all.
It wouldn't do any good for me to have it known how I
feel about my playing most of the time.

ART FARMER

The Art of Perception

Funny how you can tell the way a man's music will sound from the moment you set eyes on him. Not that this theory is infallible; an outstanding exception is the Ellington trombonist Lawrence Brown, who looks like a lawyer or at least a bored executive, never a jazzman, and then comes out on occasion with some of the funkiest horn blown this side of a New Orleans tailgate. But take Art Farmer to prove the point.

There are few musicians in jazz more poised and cultivated than the softly-spoken fluegelhorn player with the gentle manner and suave good looks. When he picks up his kingsize horn and places it carefully under that gunfighter moustache, you know he's going to play something sensitive, something carefully considered. He is one of the jazz lyricists, a virtue that is considered a trifle old-fashioned in the anything-goes contemporary ferment, yet one that at the same time gives jazz from any era the quality of timelessness. That Art is an introspective person who turns his self-examination to good purpose is obvious from every note he plays. It's quiet, peaceful music, the kind that tells of love and loving and ignores the fact that in some quarters people are trying to use it as a vehicle for hate.

It's also obvious from the way he speaks, for Art is as articulate with words as he is on his instrument. " I hope people will learn something from what I've said," was his reply concerning the significance of interviews and whether music was best left to speak for itself. " One thing they can see is that jazz musicians in general are not just dummies, unaware and unconcerned of things other than just playing jazz. The average guy comes in the club and figures the cat just goes onto the stand high and blows till he drops, goes home, wakes up at five o'clock and staggers to the nearest bar. Hell, I don't know anybody like that. But for most musicians the music remains so much more important than any other external interests. I guess we'd be out of it if we thought otherwise."

Although the fluegelhornist himself has a lively mind — he is widely read and has listened to music of all kinds — he does not consider that it is necessary for a musician to have outside interests if he is able to play what he wants to play regardless of awareness of the ways of the outside world. "But," he stressed, "it helps to be aware of different conditions and life in general. If you have an understanding of things outside music it helps you not get frustrated when things don't happen the way they should. As long as you have a knowledge of the world in general, it's some consolation. It's a good thing not to take too much too personally, because there are a lot of things we have no control over. If a person just plays music and stays as ' out ' of it as he can, drinking and making it with all the chicks he can get, that's not enough because there's a whole lot going on in the world."

For Art, the world outside the recording studio and the nightclub includes a deep appreciation of painting and an interest in politics and the sociological patterns of America. He lives with some impressive Van Gogh, Rouault and Buffet reproductions, reads avidly and listens frequently to various classical composers and the voice of Mario Lanza, rarely to jazz. Of music's many forms, he said, "You can always find something you can use some place or another. I don't think there's so much to be found in pop music apart from the occasional tune, but classical music, folk music, Eastern music — they all have something to offer. There's so much music around that the trick is to find that something you can use for yourself, something that you can feel at home in or use as a starting point for your own development. I think that the better the individual jazz musician is, the wider you'll find his range of musical appreciation to be."

Art's approach to the music is based on the exploration of melodies and is essentially an extension of his own nature. He is only at home within a lush harmonic framework and his attitude to music is the complete antithesis of the route taken by the anarchistic protagonists of the avant garde. In spite of this, he has listened shrewdly enough to the free-thinkers to appreciate their attempts at moulding a new music, whether or not he considers they succeed in their aims, and before leaving the USA in 1968 was a familiar figure at Sun Ra's experimental Monday night sessions at Slug's, the rough-and-ready home of the avant garde on New York's lower east side.

" I think that what most of them are doing is valid from their own standpoint, but only for some is it valid from the point of view of the music they are making. Some of them are being self-indulgent because it could be an easy way out, and I would like to emphasise that playing in the ' freedom ' bag without relying on preordained forms and harmonic patterns creates a good deal of responsibility as far as the artist is concerned. And it sounds to me like many people are not equipped to cope with this responsibility.

" But it doesn't matter who you play for or what you think as long as it sounds good in the end. The technique, the style — it's all meaningless compared to the final outcome of your efforts. In music the ends are more important than the means."

Speaking of a particularly candid interview he once gave, the fluegelhornist commented, " I sound so vain and stupid ! " but one of his major attributes is his ability to make candid assessments of himself and his own work. If he plays badly he knows it and no amount of praise will alter his dissatisfaction; but if he plays well, he has the ability to be, on occasion, well pleased with himself. " Some people say they never are pleased, but sometimes I go home from the job feeling very good. I know that good follows bad and bad follows good so I am able to maintain a certain amount of equilibrium. You know, if I have a bad night it doesn't bother me too much because I know that the next night will be all right."

He makes it his business to read reviews, something that few jazz musicians concerned themselves with until comparatively recently, yet the critics do not even fractionally disturb his equilibrium. " I feel that anybody is able to judge how it feels to them. My only complaint is that critics have a tendency to make allusions to the technical aspect about which they know nothing. If they'd only say, ' This didn't get to me '. Anybody is capable of saying that.

" Now there are some critics who are good for certain people. They make very good critique on the people they are able to appreciate, but it is very seldom that I've seen negative criticism that really makes it. It seems like it's easier to say why you like something than why you don't like it. Even musicians can't do this. There are only three criticisms that have ever stuck in my mind, but this doesn't mean that I think the rest is a waste of time. With such a massive production of jazz records, the jazz fan doesn't know what to buy because there's so much available. If a person is really interested and reads magazines, he'll soon find some critic who thinks the way he does and will know how to judge that critic's opinions. For instance, if you read a review on Albert Ayler by someone who likes mainstream jazz, you'll know that it doesn't have much to do with Albert Ayler. But I do wish that critics would occasionally qualify their conjectures. What they write is so often taken as dogma because the printed word is so much stronger than the sound beating on the ear. A lot of the time you see the black on white before you hear the music. So I think they should occasionally say, ' It seems to me . . .', even though you and I know that what they write is subjective."

Negative criticism has as much, if not more, value to the artist than constant, unqualified praise, feels Art. " It might not make you change your ways but at least it makes you think. It may seem pointless at the time but there is always some point in saying something. But the player himself is the most severe critic of them all. It wouldn't do any good for me to have it known how I feel about my playing most of the time. It does a person good to hear that their efforts are being appreciated even if they don't reach up to their own expectations. But if I go to work and play something I really like, I don't care what the hell anyone says or thinks about it. I'm satisfied."

To watch him working on the stand or in the studio, poised, immaculate and discreet, Art Farmer impresses as a very relaxed person. In superficial conversation he appears to be well-adjusted, not the type of musician to have any problems, yet the human element persists. " My biggest problems are completely personal : to play as I would like to play. I have thought of giving up music, but the longer you're in it the less you think of giving it up because where can you go? But it has happened in the past that I would actually put my horn in the case and store it under the bed. Nothing happened to make me change my mind, I didn't get a job or any great revelation of what I should play, I just took it out and started playing.

" I was talking to another trumpet player the other night and he said, ' Sometimes I feel like smashing it against the wall ! ' and very often I think that, too. But you never do it. For an inanimate object to get the better of you is very hard for some people to take. But you know that to smash it would be an admission of defeat and the only way to overcome it is to play it."

The outside pressures on musicians are many, especially in a club where the performer has not only to compete with the constant talking and clatter of knives and forks, but to appear professional to the audience and businesslike with the management. There are so many things to be considered, said Art, that it becomes a problem just to forget the self to the point where you are able to become totally involved in the music. " If you can do that you're no longer the little ' me ' and you block out your reactions to the music and the audience. You dedicate yourself to the music and submerge your ego. It's easy to say this, but when you get on the stand and the guy says, ' And now — Art Farmer ', I *am* Art Farmer. And if anything distracts you, you're even more conscious of being Art Farmer. But if you can react musically to situations, what comes out is going to be more true than if you go out there to react personally. You see, when you forget *yourself*, you get to the point where the music doesn't come from you, it comes through you. You become part of the total experience of ' now '. When I start thinking of ' me ', I start forcing myself, trying to play what I think I should play instead of just letting it happen.

" And when it really happens that I play what I would like to play, I don't feel a great amount of elation at being able to do it, I feel satisfaction from hearing it. But of course you have to take each night for itself. When you do something good one night you go home and you catch yourself saying, ' That's how I want to sound tomorrow ', and that's where you stub your toe and stumble."

Art's ultimate goal is to line up a string of consecutive good

nights, the kind of ambition that the impromptu nature of jazz
makes hard to realise. " But with critics, of course, they don't
often take the human element into consideration and I don't
know if they should. They come into the club or listen to a
record on the assumption that the artist is presenting something that he feels worthy of presentation — if not, why do it?
Even if he's experimenting there and then, he's still presenting
himself."

In the 1959 *Metronome* Year Book, Art Farmer was voted
one of their Musicians of the Year. " He has developed," (they
wrote), " as have nearly all the most excellent jazz artists,
out of a wealth of experience. It has given him tremendous
resources on which to draw and an adaptability which is particularly unusual in today's jazz." In the years since that was
written, he has continued to develop until there are few players
to touch him in the sphere he has chosen for his own. With his
formative years spent in the Jay McShann and Lionel Hampton big bands, and alongside such leaders as Gerry Mulligan,
Wardell Gray, Horace Silver and Lester Young, his exceptional awareness allows him to realise what he is and " where
he's at ".

" I am the sum total of what came before me, and not every
musician today is," was how he put it himself. " I don't think
you can jump through space. The quality in music can be
judged by time and good music is timeless. If it's good now,
it'll be good twenty years from now. And so I think it's stupid
for a young man to choose to play in the Dixieland way. It's
just like somebody going back to Rembrandt for painting. He
considers himself a professional painter and Rembrandt was a
great painter in his day. But I think you've got to find your
own thing and that doesn't mean to go back to so-and-so or
jump up to someone else."

In no way could Art be described as pretentious. He is a
man in enviable control of his life and his horn, and is content
to go his own musical way, developing to please himself, and
bowing and scraping to neither fad nor fashion, clubowner or
enthusiast. At times he appears as though he is standing aloof
from his fellow men because he is serious about music and
everything connected with it, but this attitude stems from a

kind of loneliness, a feeling that is often squeezed through his fluegelhorn with bittersweet poignancy. Above all, he thinks. " I think about a lot of things, not only about the notes, they're not that important. The most important thing in music is rhythm and after that comes the melody and after that, the harmony. All of it together, without something else. Music is just the expression of a human being. It's sort of a selfish thing, too. In a way, although you give, you give in order to gain satisfaction from giving."

A fleeting smile momentarily brightened the weary solemnity of his deep brown eyes. " It's just like at Christmas," he said gently, " and it's so satisfying when it's well received."

Chapter Two

Each man his own Academy

The thing that makes jazz so interesting is that each man is his own academy. . . . If he's really going to be persuasive, he learns about other academies, but the idea is that he must have that special thing. And sometimes you don't even know what it is.

CECIL TAYLOR

Each man his own Academy

Cecil Taylor and I were riding in a taxi up New York's elegant Park Avenue. The tense, elfin pianist was arguing with the driver, a crass, bloated, all-American jerk who in the course of persuading Cecil that he knew the destination better than his passenger did, addressed him as " young feller ".

" These," said Cecil with an air of bitter exasperation, " are the kind of creeps you have to deal with daily in New York City." The driver ignored this remark and slung his cab brutally into the kerb outside the sterile-looking marble and glass building that houses one of America's major television networks, unaware and uninterested that his fare was about to participate in a top-flight panel discussion with other representatives of the arts.

For the occasion Cecil had garbed his wiry frame in finely-tailored grey suiting and a yellow shirt from Carnaby Street, worn with exquisite leather riding boots. But the sight of his trim little person making his way diligently into the studio, briefcase in hand, was a far cry from the dingy apartment where he was living, sandwiched between noisy, grimy warehouses in downtown Manhattan. The incongruity of the situation, the attitude of the cabdriver, these were symptomatic of the humiliating life that a genuis whose face does not fit is forced to live.

For those who have fathomed his complex music, Cecil Taylor is a genius whose work is the jazz, or black, equivalent of straight composers like Bartok. He has become increasingly recognised in such terms by the perceptive members of the critics' fraternity, but with clubowners, who can fill the stomach more convincingly than the most lavish praise, the story is different. Those who have seen fit to dictate their own terms to him are viewed with nothing but scorn, and their dictatorial attitudes described as " that unfortunate arrogance which has no relation at all to the aesthetic reality of the musicians ". This means that there can be no communication between artist and clubowner in Cecil's world. " You have a lot to fight just to be yourself," he added dryly.

The first thing that strikes you about him is his frankly undisguised bitterness towards the society in which he lives and is forced to operate. His tight-lipped speech is occasionally tinged with a kind of sardonic humour which can be quite amusing, but at root it belongs to the " laughing just to keep from crying " of the blues. In spite of the fact that his understanding of the harmonic complexity of the music of this century has elevated him to another plateau in the eyes of his admirers, the pianist has operated in all the areas of jazz music and remains a bluesman at heart, whatever label the critics care to pin on him.

Earlier, he had been talking about the music of John Cage, a composer he admires yet whose influence on modern non-jazz composers is, he feels, too total and has inhibited further creativity on their part. " He's interesting, God, he's the most interesting musician in terms of ideas, but the music that's resulting from it is indicative of something that's very dangerous, something very in vogue in the most austere circles in New York City."

He was, indirectly, referring to the dilettantish cliques that had recently adopted him, an out-of-work illegitimate, but in the television discussion in which he was about to take part, the talk would probably be on the usual effete level and the cap would doubtless fit there equally well. " If you get to know or feel the emotional fibres of these people and you listen to them talk, the talk is always very quiet, very soft and refined, and the taste, oh, the finest taste in books and so on. They're very gentle, they look so pale and anaemic, but they're very bright and they're very witty, and they can't do much of anything really. They can think, but they don't *live*! " He hissed the words : " There's no fucking *blood*! "

The bitterness persisted during his discourse on the followers of Cage. " You have the really hip ones who destroy instruments as a ' happening '. You have scores which from the point of view of tradition have been expanded to incorporate, like, the idea of improvisation, but, of course, because Mr Cage is an American with the sense of 'closedness' of Americans, he couldn't call that 'improvisation' and make one think of one's black citizen brothers."

Cecil laughed mirthlessly. "You have to invent a series of games to obscure the fact that essentially what you're doing is asking musicians to 'improvise'. Well, unfortunately, most of the so-called classical musicians in this country — except organ players — have not had any background in improvisation. The other idea is that because the jazz thing has come so that the geniuses have for the most part been black, the idea is that you cannot really accept them improvising because you cannot really accept the idea of black being in any way equal.

"Music is really organisation of sound and every man is entitled to his means of how that sound is arrived at — but only if you think of him as a man. So, of course, Charlie Parker never *created* any music, you understand, after all he just picked notes out of the air. It wasn't the practising of licks or a spiritual catharsis which resulted in the choice of particular tones, that couldn't have happened."

The vigorous intensity of Cecil's music, which is also reflected in the way he talks, is unmatched by anyone playing jazz today with the possible exception of Ornette Coleman. That such furore should emanate from a non-sustaining instrument like the piano is more than a little unusual. Cecil has a unique facility for sustaining improvisation at the white-heat level and rarely lets up until he is exhausted both physically and emotionally.

He is totally dedicated to his music and has always been so, according to those who have known him since the late 'fifties when he first began to be noticed in his native New York. The critical reaction to his first quartet, which included the soprano saxophonist Steve Lacy, was mixed. Some recognised his genius from the first, others loathed what he was doing, but now most people concede his importance even if they don't especially like what he is doing. Few, in fact, are the musicians who would put him down. Cecil is an exceptionally candid man with no qualms about telling the truth and little sympathy for those who are unable to appreciate his often impenetrable musical form.

" It's all right by me," is the way he blithely reacts to rejection. " It's, like, I'm doing my homework and it's up to everybody else who's really interested in the evolvement of the art (as well as the kick they might get from it) to do theirs."

He allowed that the listener " must, I suppose, like it very much to take the trouble ", adding that he, personally, shies away from whatever he finds distasteful. His uncompromising attitude is very understandable, stemming as it does from the days of his youth when his mother would stand over the piano, ruler in hand, ready to rap his fingers any time he made a mistake. " In a sense I've made, like, the complete trip from that discipline and the ruler and the whole bit to none of that. So music isn't a matter of work, it isn't a matter of, like, studying, it's a matter of grooving, of doing things because I like to do them."

It is nothing new for the members of any avant garde to be shouted down as charlatans, and in jazz the outcry is often more vocal than in other spheres. However, as Cecil clearly pointed out, the financial rewards are so sparse for those involved in experimentation that he would be a masochist if sincerity were not the driving force behind the explorations of himself and his confrères. " Even though we may not dig their sound spectrum, through the fact that they make, like, consistent noises in a certain direction of playing, or, like, volume, over a certain amount of years, it must occur finally to someone that not only are these people serious, but that there is no other way open to them. Because, Jesus, if this is a materialistic society and you're a member of the so-called avant garde (they even have a little category which means that you're even more exclusively a minority inside a minority), it means you have nothing.

" You don't even have what passes for communion from your musical community, you don't even have that. Your isolation is pretty complete and you certainly don't get any support from a family. Most of the cats have to support families, so there is no reason for us to have done this unless, of course, we actually believed in it. No, no one wants to have a hard time making it."

Not only does Cecil work infrequently, he is one of the most

elusive of New York's musicians. You could, as I did, call him
every day for a week and not find him at home. His interests
range from poetry to the ballet and whenever he is not
immersed in his piano, he is more than likely to be walking
in the park, talking with writers and painters or at the opera,
" grooving ". He lives in surroundings that echo what someone
once said of Tennessee Williams : " he looked like a man who
had dropped in to visit himself ". Empty coffee-cups, unmatched socks and heavily-scored manuscript paper jostle with
pens, pencils, books of poetry and a half-dozen vests and pants
inside the lid of his open piano. For those whom his music
unsettles, such chaotic surroundings would seem to be an
accurate reflection of his musical personality, yet Cecil Taylor
exists above and in spite of the chaos. He is a fascinating artist,
an unselfconscious intellectual whose penetrating conversation
is apt to take the most unexpected turns in order to keep up
with his fertile mind.

Cecil was born in Long Island City in 1933. The first pianist
he heard was an uncle who played in a stride style, " very
ornate and very delicate ", and who also gave him a few drum
lessons. " Among the names, it's hard to say, but I've always
liked Fats Waller. As a child I suppose you like these people
partly because they're entertaining or bizarre or strange, sort
of like a bad dream or a very funny dream, and Fats was
always funny. I remember him playing ' Honeysuckle Rose '
once and hearing the kind of impulse that the piano had, or
impulses separate from *pulse*, you know. Everything he did
seemed to be done before it actually was done and it seemed
to colour everything that the other musicians were doing.
There was this kind of feedback, and I suppose it was really
my first awareness of the kind of exchange that happens
between jazz musicians."

His mother came from New Jersey and had grown up with
the former Duke Ellington drummer, Sonny Greer, so that
Duke was " very much a part of the family by-laws ". His own
piano style stems, by way of Thelonious Monk, from Ellington.
" Well, I think it's in the tradition." He is, nevertheless, a
totally unique pianist who has only been superficially copied
and there seems to be little danger of his being outdistanced.

Originality often stems from a musician's growing up cut off from readily available influences, and in Cecil's case his own contacts with music were limited. " Then it goes into another stage when maybe you go to school for a while and are exposed to all those influences and for a while you don't know exactly where you are. But then, of course, the old self comes back. The thing that makes jazz so interesting is that each man is his own academy. By and large, if he's really going to be persuasive, he learns about other academies, but the idea is that he must have that special thing. And sometimes you don't even know what it is."

During the early 'fifties, Cecil attended the New England Conservatory of Music in Boston and, on graduation, returned to New York for the long hard winter of discontent into which a pale sun has only lately shone. Work in the clubs was so scarce as to be almost non-existent and the pianist was forced to seek alternative employment. " Jobs? Oh, you can count 'em on many hands! " The turning point came in 1962 when he was working as a dishwasher in a restaurant where, by the cruel irony peculiar to New York, records by Ornette Coleman, John Coltrane and himself were played daily. " I decided, well, this work difficulty is a by-product of your stamp and you must either face this and make it work, or nothing. So I used to practise like six hours a day before I came to work and that solved the problem for a while."

Through practice Cecil attained a new confidence in himself and decided to approach a " terrible coffee-shop owner " and more or less demand employment. " He wanted someone else and I don't know how I did it, but I talked him into giving us a trial. I guess the only way I was able to pull it off was because I felt that I was so *right*, that anyone having to suffer all that shit *must* be, and so I convinced him. There were, of course, many nights when we earned maybe a dollar for the trio, but we worked there for something like thirteen weeks and really learned something." This engagement was, in a way, the start of Cecil's minimally increasing fortunes. When he closed there he took a group to Europe for a while, though on his return there were few open arms waiting to greet him.

The most dominant characteristic of his music is its energy.

An average set can last non-stop for over an hour, the pianist directing events from the keyboard, his fingers seemingly tearing at the keys to make the instrument spew forth its guts in convolute slabs of sound. You can almost see him sweating blood as he lunges into the heart of the music, totally involved with the piano. This incredible energy of Cecil's stems initially, he says, from relaxation, " the feeling that your body will do whatever you want it to. You've got to just sit there and then, of course, the music really takes over."

If, said Cecil, you have spent twenty years of your life so immersed in something that even when you are not physically involved in it you are gathering material to fuel the fire, " each piece is, in a sense, a problem. It has certain technical aspects that, like, differentiate it from the next piece you play, but since it is not only a matter of technique but a matter of the shape of the piece being arrived at because one you loved liked the sound of it and you enjoyed doing it, what is going to happen? How are *they* going to react to it? That's why, even before I became aware of what was happening with me, I always had trouble with guys, with clubowners who said ' You play too much ' and ' too long ', their conception of time being regimented along machine-shop lines. They think about making their money but they will not grant me the same concern. They say ' You ask too much ', so you see it's not accidental that we didn't record for three years or were not heard in New York clubs for four."

The hazards of non-compromise are many. That Cecil has navigated the worst of them is evident from his continuing creativity and indicative of his perseverance. Yet only once has he been in a position to actually turn down a fairly substantial offer, " and this was very much to the point that this clubowner was trying to be responsible for the shaping of jazz, in a very negative way." In 1965, at the end of a successful five weeks at the Village Vanguard (" we were booked for two weeks and he asked us to come back for three "), the owner told Cecil : " I want you to come back as a piano soloist."

Cecil's laugh had a hysterical edge. " I mean, with no musical experience ! But it's not just about me playing the piano, it's about my inter-relatedness with the piano. In effect the man was telling me, ' I want your music to be thus ' or ' I want this to happen ' in terms of its formal aspect! He was prepared to offer me a good salary for the year, working the club on a regular basis, and this salary he offered was not fantastic but good. It was well above the average layman's salary. I mean, in thirteen weeks you can make more than the, let's say, ' upper middle class ' make in a year. And I couldn't do it. I was enraged, as a matter of fact."

It would not be inappropriate to describe his music as " enraged " for in it the cry of the misunderstood is vividly heard. But it is not just Cecil's own frustration that is so vehemently vocalised, it is the cry of today. " The scenes that are going on in America right now — political, social and economic — these are much more important than any kind of physical involvement with your instrument. Shutting your mind to the happenings was the final bankruptcy that the academy left us with, the current life in America *now* is the material for artists."

Chapter Three

Lock the fox

If you possess this quality, to create, you can apply it to some other craft. You don't become dormant just because you've stopped playing.

EDDIE ''LOCKJAW'' DAVIS

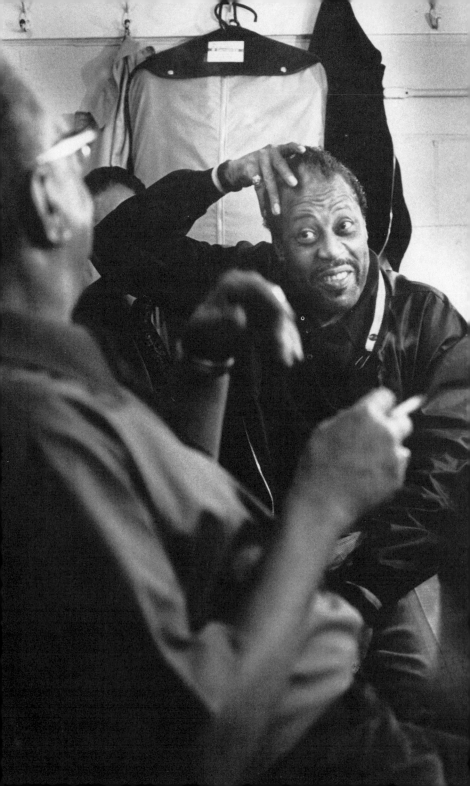

Lock the fox

Eddie "Lockjaw" Davis possesses not only the immobile embouchure which earned him his soubriquet, but a countenance which is possibly the most blasé in a world where most eyes have seen it all. To say that the saxophonist's expression is world-weary would be putting it mildly, yet when he starts muscling in on a tune, his big, blustery tenor sound gives the lie to his singularly jaundiced appearance. The immediately recognisable Davis saxophone is as lusty as the jazz life itself. Honking, stomping and sinuous, it's a meaty charge right out of the mainstream of jazz.

" Jaws ", whose acute powers of observation and a compulsion to get to the heart of any given subject would make him an outstanding individual in any walk of life, is unique in a field where the majority of people tend to drift with the tide and seldom question the whys and wherefores of the structure of the business. " I've been accused many times by club proprietors, promoters, record people, and so on : ' You're not like the typical musician ', but that's because they've never really taken the time to talk to different musicians," declared Lockjaw. " Musicians are like any other individual who creates or improvises — they are individuals, you cannot categorise them. You cannot say, ' They're all the same '. Each one has a different personality just as he has a different style of playing, so anyone who deals with them must view them individually — and that can be quite a job."

It's a job which the saxophonist himself undertook when he hung up his horn after more than twenty years of bandstands and dancehalls and temporarily exchanged the rigours of the road for the nine-till-five of the office desk. As a sideman in the section, as leader of his own combo, as road manager and featured soloist with Count Basie, and as a booker for one of the largest agencies in America, Jaws has had a unique opportunity to assess the business from every side.

When things go wrong on the gig — and, by virtue of the unpredictable nature of jazz, its audience and performers, this is a far from rare occurrence — tradition has it that the artist blames the promoter for the failure and vice versa. Few have the desire or the ability to be objective or concede that any factor apart from the other's unadaptability could be the cause of a setback. Read any interview with musicians and you'll find that there's always something wrong with the monsters who live to exploit the poor jazzmen, but few have had Eddie Davis's chance to be on both sides of the fence.

" In booking musicians into clubs it is often the agent who is to blame for what becomes a vicious spiral," he pointed out, and gave this illustration : " A new clubowner opens a club and calls you up as an agent and says ' I'd like to get So-and-so.' Now you are an eager agent with designs on getting the most out of as little work as possible and so you over-sell your artist.

" Say that your artist generally sells for 1,000 dollars and you ask for 1,500. The new owner doesn't know, he buys it, and suddenly you've created a Frankenstein. Number one, the room is not going to be able to support that kind of money so therefore the clubowner is going to lose money on his first venture. Number two, the artist feels that if you can get 1,500 from this john you can get it from every other and so this is his new price. Thirdly, you're going to lose that account because through over-selling the artist can't work and finally he's going to be hard to get along with because he can't understand working under 1,500 anywhere."

The performer, stated Lockjaw, is generally accused of pricing himself out of the business, instead of the blame being laid at his agent's door. " In most cases the artist doesn't even know of the transaction ! Now when he makes the job and ' dies ', he doesn't feel that it's his fault, he feels that it's because the people don't know about him yet, or the clubowner didn't advertise him properly and so forth. The next go-wrong is when the agent tries to give this price to another clubowner. He tells the guy that the artist won't budge from 1,500, so in other words the agent is in a position to either make or break a fellow."

The agent is also in a position to get the best co-operation from an artist, and one of the main factors in destroying a career is what he termed " a drastic man shortage in the agency business. It's because so many eager beavers want to get rich quick. They don't have the compassion for the business, they have no desire to struggle along and build up something, all they want to do is make money."

From this vicious circle of events, explained Lockjaw, musicians will inevitably shed their agents and eventually start trying to sell themselves. " That's what we call ' emergency gigs '," he smiled. " They feel like they're getting away with something but in actual fact they're taking way less than their normal money. But at least when they get it, it's all theirs."

When Davis joined Shaw Artists Corporation in June 1963, he took with him an exceptional knowledge of some aspects of the business and a ready, willing and able attitude to learn the rest. During his three years with the agency, he took the time to look around and absorb the incongruities of the agency game. " I discovered that many agents have never seen some of the rooms they book, many agents have never seen the artist work. They just get on the phone and say ' This is a great artist ! ' He's only interested in his commission, so what happens? Catastrophe ! This is why rooms are closing down all over America — in part. I'm not going to give them all the blame because many artists have helped kill it, too, by their conduct and so on."

Reverting to the subject of the musicians who are now demanding more money than they can possibly hope to get, Lockjaw related that they subsidise their existence by the " new vogue ", teaching. " Those who have any name quality can easily acquire certain aspirational musicians who want to advance and this is the nucleus of their income," he said. " Maybe three or four of them will open a studio and that, together with their gigs around town, is how they survive. They work out that they can make more that way than running out of town all the time and involving themselves in transportation costs."

This, in turn, is making it harder and harder for " name "

musicians who want to go on the road to assemble the sidemen of their choice. Jaws discovered this for himself when he
returned to active playing after his agency stint. " The first
question I was asked was, ' Will you be going out of town? '
and when I asked why, they'd say, ' Well, I have some students,
you know.' And then their price to work *in* town was astro-
nomical. If I'd been stupid enough to pay it, they'd have taken
it. In other words, the spirit of music and of working together
with So-and-so on drums has gone. It's all economics now. So
I abandoned the thought immediately because if I'd have
hired the musicians I had in mind, I'd have ended up making
nothing. And they weren't joking."

The majority of students derive, ironically, from the rock-
and-roll field which has been busily trying to kill jazz since
the early 'fifties. " Anyone from a rock group who has made
it now wants to become a good staunch musician. So who does
he turn to? Not the so-called ' instructor ', he wants the name
jazz musician to teach him and he's in a position to pay. It is
very lucrative."

What is most decidedly not lucrative today, and has never
been for anyone other than the relatively notable leader who
can command a higher price for his services, is the whole
business of taking a jazz combo on the road. Every musician
is responsible for his own food and accommodation, but the
leader must take care of transport and any taxes that might be
incurred. " If he's going to travel by car, naturally he has a
big car or two station wagons," explained the saxophonist,
himself a man who has put in many hours behind the wheel.
" It's just a question of who's driving. Very few small groups
fly, only on jazz festivals where the promoter is furnishing
transportation. Generally trips are made by car, so you just
try to keep the mileage decent. You try not to do 2,000 miles
overnight! "

The exorbitant taxes that a bandleader is expected to pay
today are another reason why more and more groups are
quitting the road and why " name " soloists prefer to work as
" singles " with a local rhythm section. " The leader used to
pay a ten per cent travelling tax for his sidemen, but this has
been revoked. Now they have a thing called work dues for

which each individual is liable, but the sideman generally gets around this by stating his salary plus an additional amount of money to cover this. So, technically, the leader is still paying that."

Lockjaw went on to break down the economics of touring, listing further deductions which include federal income tax, state tax, social security and even the newly introduced city tax. He pointed out that if a sideman plays an afternoon matinée or record date while technically under someone's leadership and fails to declare it, the leader will be held responsible and may have to pay up to five times the amount due in interest and penalty. "For instance, if you hire your friend and he refuses to have you deduct taxes out of his money, you might value his services to the point where you would rather have him and you figure out that you can get away with it. The whole thing has gotten ridiculous in the States."

Little, if any, reading between the lines is needed to see why Jaws chose to relinquish the dubious joys of leading his own group for the humdrum round of telephone, diary, route book and desk. Nevertheless, he maintained, there were other reasons. "When I used to look around and see some of the elder statesmen of jazz and see the age at which they still had to play, I couldn't envision that as regards to *my* future," he said. "I thought it was unfortunate that a musician who had given so many devoted years to a craft or trade had nothing else to learn and so had no other choice but to continue playing in order to sustain himself.

"I felt that the time to make a change is while you're still active, to start learning another craft while you're still in the public's eye, so I decided to try to get into the administrative part. I didn't feel it was timely to wait until I was bedridden or handicapped!"

Lockjaw spent over two years with Shaw Artists Corporation, familiarising himself with every aspect of the booking of both jazz and rock-and-roll performers into widely differing venues. Although the two camps are a little more integrated in the United States than they are in Europe, the saxophonist-turned-booker found that having to acquaint himself with the rock-and-roll setup came as quite a challenge because of his jazz background. " I've always believed that the better he knows his product, the better the salesman," said he sagely. And ever-ready Eddie made it his business to get to know most of the artists he was handling and to familiarise himself with their respective idioms. He discovered that you learn the feeling of responsibility when working in a field where your own income is based on the bonus system.

" In other words, you like to see a room prosperous and so you make decisions as to whether to sell a club an artist just to make a commission or whether it's more important to keep the club open. Like in any other craft, you have a lot of eager beavers who are not interested in the club's lifetime, only in their own immediate needs. Therefore, the club is sometimes buying artists that do them no good and do the artist no good, either. I advocated long ago that the agencies need more people with some experience of musicianship, people who know some of the conditions, some of the needs and wants of both sides."

In the sagacious Eddie Davis, the agency game temporarily held a unique ace-in-the-hole, but when in November 1964 Count Basie asked the saxophonist to rejoin him in the capacity of road manager, his enquiring mind considered that such a move would link him directly with yet another side of the administration. The thankless task of road manager is a much-maligned occupation, yet without these alert and ever-minstering guardian angels, the show would very often not go on. Not only was Lockjaw the jack-of-all-trades responsible for handling the payroll, transportation and accommodation reservations, he had to act as wet nurse to the musicians and make sure they turned up at rehearsals, drunk or sober, and were never left behind when the band moved on. To cap this responsibility, it was suggested after a couple of weeks on the road that he resume active playing. " This," said he laconically, " aroused my interest considerably because it also entailed two salaries."

His saxophone had been left at home in the basement — " a trophy for all my guests to see " — but when Jaws sent home for the instrument his move sparked off considerable resentment from his fellow sidemen. " The musicians didn't like it," he stated flatly. " First, they felt that here was a musician who was aware of what they were making because each member of the orchestra has an individual salary, and secondly, they resented me being in possession of a lot of advance information such as band itineraries and so on. As a whole I had too much authority for their liking."

Most of this resentment came from the orchestra's older members, who felt that their seniority should have recommended them for a better-paying job. " Although," smiled Lockjaw easily, " that wasn't the point." In the end, however, most differences were ironed out by the saxophonist commanding respect because he respected the others as individuals. " Since I've left the orchestra I've never discussed anything personal regarding the musicians, be it their salaries or their attitudes, because I feel that after you leave an orchestra, you leave the business segment with it."

Lockjaw, who learns continually from every new endeavour he undertakes, insists that being a personal manager or road manager requires a great deal of patience and understanding but, above all, mutual respect. " Once you respect a musician, he in turn respects you," he pointed out. " Dealing with a creative person is a little bit different to dealing with somebody on the assembly line. The average musician has a self-built-in pride, because it's the only occupation where the individual is aware of his limitations without anyone telling him. It's the only craft where you don't have to be told what you can and what you can't do because you're aware of that before anyone else."

Although Lockjaw believes strongly that the attitude " once a musician, always a musician " is merely a myth, he has carried on as an active participant on the creative side of the fence. He frequently stresses that he has never been " *that* hooked on playing " and that he can take it or leave it, but at the same time he reveals that the reason so many musicians stick with their horns in spite of the problems in the day-to-day jazz life is because they have what he fondly called " a certain compassion for the business ".

He elucidated : " It's something they like to do. You must

remember that the hours you put into the job compared to the daily worker are much less. At best you've got to put in five hours. Then there are the outside things to be gained. While you're working on one job, someone will come up and offer you a record date or another little gig, whereas if you were on a day job, you'd only have the one basic income. In other words, in spite of all the taxes and so on, it's a job with opportunities that the layman doesn't have. There's always something extra."

And in accordance with the philosophy that in the final assessment you give back what you've received, the majority of jazz musicians usually manage to insert that little extra something into their music, even when the deal is against them. For all his outward veneer of disenchantment and cynicism, the lethargic original with the unlikely nickname is no exception. Homespun philosopher and impudent improviser, dogmatist and wistful would-be commentator on world affairs, Eddie Lockjaw Davis is a man amongst men.

Chapter Four

Round about Monk

Let 'em laugh, they need something to laugh at. . . .
Somebody got something to say about everything you do.

THELONIOUS MONK

Round about Monk

Thelonious Sphere Monk is not the kind of name you'd easily forget. As someone once sagely remarked: " With a name like that he was made from an early age — all he needed was a hustle."

In Monk's case the chosen commodity was music. One of the outstanding composers and pianists that jazz has produced, he is also that rare entity, a true jazz original. Although his methods of composition have had a profound and lasting influence on the course of contemporary jazz, Monk is unique in having attracted no legion of slavish imitators. As he himself chooses to explain it in his laconic manner: " Musicians play my tunes but they can't play my style. They try to, you know. . . . Some of my things are hard. They're hard in all kind of ways."

Monk (very few people actually call him Thelonious or even Sphere) fits the conventional picture of the jazz eccentric a little too closely for comfort. The first oddity to inspire comment is his famous choice of hats, their size and diversity of style; the fact that the capricious pianist is rarely seen on or off the bandstand without some splendid piece of headgear perched on top of his magnificent, full-bearded head. But whether it be fez, turban or just a plain old-fashioned cloth cap, Monk strenuously protests at the popular notion that he actually sleeps in his hat. He is, nevertheless, an erratic being with a complete disregard for time, eating and sleeping when and where the mood takes him. Because of his well-known unreliability and the length of time taken by the jazz public to catch up with his musical directions, times in the past have been bad for the eccentric genius and the work all but nonexistent.

Now, at last, it's Monk's time. He's famous now. He appears in glossy magazines, wears 150-guinea suits and stays at the best hotels. But as his wife Nellie says : " He's no more impressed with himself than he was in the dark days."

Music is his life, and he appears to be concerned with little else outside it, himself and his family. If he ever thinks of the way of the world, he rarely shows it. Speaking of Monk the composer, Quincy Jones, once summed it up : " Thelonious is one of the main influences in modern jazz composition, but he is not familiar with many classical works, or with much life outside himself, and I think because of this he did not create on a contrived or inhibited basis."

The Mad Monk, the High Priest of Bebop — Monk has been called many things through the years he struggled for acceptance, but one title for which he will never qualify is that of the most articulate conversationalist in jazz. An interview with him takes patience, so few people have bothered. The majority of lay journalists who have been understandably intrigued by this ready-made wayward bohemian tend to give up trying after a dozen or so false starts and rely on mentioning the times he was billed to appear at a club and never showed; then leave it at that. But he has his mellow days. I got Monk to speak.

" I started to take up trumpet as a kid but I didn't play it," he began tentatively when we met during a visit to London. " I always wanted to play the piano and jazz appealed to me. I just like every aspect of it, you can try so many things with jazz. I was about eleven or something like that when I started and I used to play with all the different side-bands when I was a teenager."

Did he ever think he might become a world-famous jazz pianist? " Well, that's what I was aimin' at ! "

When Monk plays, you can almost hear him thinking out loud as he selects a note and carefully considers its effect before adding a couple of others, judiciously chosen. Although he received a conventional formal training, Monk plays " incorrectly ", with his fingers held parallel to the keyboard, gently shaping the keys to his thoughts. But he doesn't stab at the keys in the way that some people imagine. It's a flowing thing.

Was he ever taught to hold his hands in the formal manner?

" That's how you're supposed to? " he asked, feigning wide-
eyed surprise. " I hold them any way I feel like holding 'em.
I hit the piano with my elbow sometimes because of a certain
sound I want to hear, certain chords. You can't hit that many
notes with your hands. Sometimes people laugh when I'm
doing that. Yeah, let 'em laugh! They need something to
laugh at."

Monk lived at home off and on until his marriage to his
childhood friend and neighbour, the indefatigable Nellie. This
is a rather unusual pattern for a jazz musician, but Monk
firmly dismisses the suggestion. " I don't know what other
people are doing; I just know about me. I cut out from home
when I was a teenager and went on the road for about two
years."

His mother, who was particularly proud of her well-behaved
son, sang in the choir at the local Baptist church in New York
City where the family lived. Whenever she had a leading part,
the young Thelonious would go along and accompany her on
piano. She, in turn, would visit the dives where he worked.
" My mother never figured I should do anything else. She was
with me. If I wanted to play music, it was all right with her,
and Nellie is the same way.

" Yeah, I played in the Baptist church and I'll tell you
something else. I worked with the Evangelists for some time,
too. The music I played with them seems to be coming out
today. They're playing a lot of it now. I did about two years
all over the States; playing in the churches was a lot of fun.
When I got through, I'd had enough of church, though. I was
in there practically every night. But I always did play jazz.
In the churches I was playing music the same way. I wouldn't
say I'm religious, but I haven't been around the churches in
a good while now so I don't know what they're putting down
in there now."

Of Minton's, the Harlem club long held to be the incubator
of bop, Monk, like others of his fellow iconoclasts of the time
who played there, declared that the music " just happened. I
was playing there, so the others just used to come down and
play with me. I guess they dug what I was doing. It was
always crowded there, people enjoying themselves all the time.

What I was doing was just the way I was thinking. I wasn't thinking about trying to change the course of jazz, I was just trying to play something that sounded good. I never used to talk about it with other people, but I believe the other musicians did. It just happened."

For a long time he found it difficult to obtain work, but with typical Monkish nonchalance he says, " I didn't notice it too much. I had certain things to do. I wasn't starving or nothing." Nellie, whom he married in 1947, was a great help and comfort through the lean years. She worked at a variety of clerical jobs and when she was pregnant with their first child, Thelonious Jr., used to take in sewing. " Music to him is work," she said. " When he wasn't working regularly, he'd be working at home, writing and rehearsing bands that didn't have the prospects of a dog. He just did it to know what it'd sound like. In the ' un ' years, as I call them, as far as he was concerned, he felt just as confident as he does now that what he was doing musically could appeal to other people if only they took the opportunity to listen.

" We live music every day. Thelonious has never attempted to do anything else except play music. He's always been optimistic." Her husband confirmed this : " How can I be anything other than what I am ? "

To date Monk has composed almost sixty tunes, some of the best known being " Round Midnight ", " Blue Monk ", " Rhythm-n-ing ", and the first modern jazz classic, " Epistrophy ", which was written in collaboration with Kenny Clarke, then the Minton's house-drummer. He claims he has no particular favourite among his many compositions and that the unusual names for many of his tunes " just come to me ". Sometimes he composes at the piano, though more often than not he has a melody running around in his head. Although he said, " You have to stay home and relax to write the music ", his wife commented that " he thinks about music all the time he's not talking. He may be able to compose in a room full of people, just standing there. I don't know anybody else who can just withdraw like that. He has a marvellous capacity for withdrawal."

This withdrawal includes not speaking to his wife for days

on end, " unless he wants me to fetch something ", and she will only break the silence if she has something urgent to tell him. " Even then he might not reply or show that he's heard," she said, " but in emergencies his reactions are very fast. He's more contained than most people and, therefore, more helpful than someone who falls apart and goes to pieces."

When he is writing, Monk said, he does not think of the actual notes or of the effect his finished work will have on his audience. " I'm just thinking about the music," he added. " You think about everything else automatically. I think about what anyone else does." And what does he think of the public? " I think very highly of the public. I think they're capable of knowing if something sounds all right. I figure that if it sounds all right to me, it sounds all right to them."

Jazz musicians are by nature itinerants who usually spend the best part of their lives moving around. But Monk, always the individualist, prefers to stay in New York City as much as possible. He has lived in a small, undistinguished apartment on West Sixty-third Street for the past thirty years and he is very attached to his home. " There's nothing special about it," he said, " but I guess I'll always keep it."

He once remarked that if he couldn't be in New York he'd rather be on the moon, but he denies this tongue-in-cheek statement. " Did I say that? Can't remember it. I don't know anything about what's happening on the moon but I know what's happening in New York. I like New York City, I haven't been anywhere that tops it yet."

Does he listen to the sounds of New York? " Yeah, I have to; I live there. I wasn't born there but I've been living there all my life." (Monk was born in Rocky Mount, North Carolina.) " You can't shut the sound out too easily; you always hear some kind of noise going on. I guess all sort of things have an effect on what you're writing. But I was raised in New York, it's home to me. That's what I dig about it. You want to know what sounds I put into my music — well, you have to go to New York to listen for yourself. I can't describe them. How do you expect me to describe to you right here how New York sounds? How does London sound? Can you tell me how it sounds — huh? "

On stage Monk will often rise from the piano stool and stand listening intently to the other soloists, swaying slightly in what has been termed a " rhythmic dance ". He gets exasperated when people comment on such aspects of his personal behaviour. " What's that I'm supposed to be doing? " he demanded. " I get tired sitting down at the piano! That way I can dig the rhythm better. Somebody's got something to say about everything you do!

" I miss a lot of things that're written about me. I don't read papers, I don't read magazines. Of course, I'm interested in what's going on in music, but I'm not interested in what somebody else is writing or anything like that. I don't let that bug me. In fact, I don't see those ' columns ' or whatever you call 'em. People write all kinds of jive.

" I've got a wife and two kids to take care of, and I have to make some money and see that they eat and sleep, and me, too — you dig? What happens 'round the corner, what happens to *his* family is none of my business. I have to take care of my family. But I'll help a lot of people, and I have. . . . But I don't go around. . . . What's the matter with you? No! I'm not interested in what's happening nowhere. Are you worried about what's happening to everybody? Why do you ask me that? Why should I be worried? *You're* not! Why do you ask me a stupid question like that — something that you don't dig yourself? I don't *be* around the corner, looking into everybody's house, looking to see what's happening. I'm not a policeman or a social worker — that's for your social workers to do. I'm not in power. I'm not worrying about politics. *You* worry about the politics. Let the statesmen do that — that's their job. They get paid for it. If you're worried about it, stop doing what you're doing! "

And just as he refuses to concern himself with politics, Monk is, on the surface, equally indifferent towards racial problems. " I hardly know anything about it," he said, brushing the subject aside. " I never was interested in those Muslims. If you want to know, you should ask Art Blakey. I didn't have to change my name — it's always been weird enough! I haven't done one of those ' freedom ' suites, and I don't intend to. I mean, I don't see the point. I'm not thinking that race thing now, it's not on my mind. Everybody's trying to get me to think it, though, but it doesn't bother me. It only bugs the people who're trying to get me to think it."

Monk is an extremely self-willed person. Rarely does he do anything that does not interest him. He seldom goes to parties and when he is neither working nor walking around Manhattan, a favourite pastime, he is at home with Nellie and their two children, Thelonious Jr. and Barbara. Now, past fifty, he seems hardly aware of the substantial increase in his income in recent years and says that money makes no difference to his way of life. " If I feel like it, I'll spend it," he said, " but I spend it on what anybody else spends it on — clothes and food. My wife and kids spend a lot of money, but I really don't know how much I make. I'd go stupid collecting and counting my money. I worked at seventeen dollars a week when I was a kid, make thousands now. At fourteen, fifteen years old I could do anything I wanted with that money. It wasn't bad for that age. I really don't want to do anything else other than what I'm doing. I like playing music. Everything's all right. I don't look like I'm worrying about anything, do I? I don't talk much because you can't tell everybody what you're thinking. Sometimes you don't know what you're thinking yourself ! "

A faithfully perceptive wife, Nellie added : " You wouldn't know whether he was happy or not at any time. He's always been very agreeable. Even in the direst situations you can't see if he's worried from looking at his face. Maybe you can tell from a chance remark, but he isn't a worrier. We have a theory that worry creates a mental block and prevents you from being creative. So worry is a waste of time."

When he is not working or enjoying family life, the pianist likes to walk around. He will sometimes stand for hours on the corner of West Sixty-third Street, just thinking about music. Everyone in the neighbourhood knows who he is, but Monk speaks rarely to passers-by. And when he starts to walk, " I just walk and dig." He and Nellie also belong to America's vast army of television addicts. " I haven't been to the movies in a long time," he admitted. " I look at TV, see everything there just laying in the bed. You have to get up and go to movies, where you fall asleep in your chair. That way you're in bed already. But I never get enough sleep. I haven't slept eight hours through in a long time."

Does he ever get a vacation? " Not with pay ! "

In the years when Monk found it hard to make his musical mark he once hit the headlines in a more sensational manner when he was arrested on a charge of possessing marijuana. The drug had apparently been planted in his car and he was released from jail after only a few days, but the story, being part of the sinister image of the jazz musician, stuck. " Being in jail is a drag," Monk recalled ruefully. " I'm sorry for anybody that's in jail. I was only in for a few days and that's been so long ago, but, you know. . . . In the United States the police bothers you more than they do anywhere else. The police heckle you more. You don't have that much trouble anywhere else in the world except the United States. The police just mess with you for nothing. They just bully people and all that kind of shit. They carry guns, too, and they shoot people for nothing.

" New York violent? It has to be violent if the cops are making the trouble. They pick on anybody. I don't be worrying about it any longer but they'll start trouble with you if they want to. They don't talk to you nice, they talk to you any kind of way. You don't run into trouble so much if you're kind of famous, but people that is kinda down, they just pick on them. But New York changes. Any place changes a lot because you have different generations coming up with new ideas. The police ain't quite as bad as they used to be, but they'd probably get better if they put more intelligent people on the force."

Monk is noncommittal about his favourite composers and musicians. " I listen to 'em all," he says, yet it is hard to believe that he ever goes out of his way to listen to the music of other people. One evidence of this could be that his own work is so self-contained, so very personal, but he finds little time to add to his repertoire today. He continually records the same tunes (" so somebody will hear 'em "), and when asked to bring a new Monk tune to one particular recording session, turned up with the hymn " Abide With Me " which, he blandly informed the assembled company, was written by one William H. Monk. It was recorded.

For the last ten years or so, Monk's music has become easier to listen to, though it is not necessarily any simpler. What he is doing is as engaging as ever, though far less provocative than when he was upsetting the rules.

"If you think my playing is more simple, maybe that's because you can dig it better," Monk said and laughed. "It takes that long for somebody to hear it, I guess. I mean for them to understand it or for you to get to them for them to hear it, because you might be changing and then stop playing, and they'd not get a chance to hear it."

The massive, bearded figure leaned back in his chair and grinned expansively. "But," he added, "I never be noticing these things; I just be trying to play." He sank back into an untidy heap, looking for all the world like a huge, well-dressed grizzly bear who had somehow found a home in the recesses of a plushly padded armchair at the London Hilton. For Monk, it was time, indisputably *his* time. He closed his eyes. He slept.

Chapter Five

A lesson in lovemaking

You're not supposed to *rape* the drums, you make love to
them as far as I'm concerned !

BILLY HIGGINS

A lesson in lovemaking

"You're not supposed to *rape* the drums, you make love to them as far as I'm concerned!" The gregarious Billy Higgins, who has played drums for just about everybody out here, was actively criticising the loudness and lack of control that separates the boys from the men in jazz percussion today.

The outburst was rather out of character for the skinny little drummer who moves and grooves in his own sweet way and is inclined to avoid any serious discussion. Billy would rather turn you off with a disarmingly cheeky grin or a drawling line in hip talk than actually get into a conversation, yet he is exceptionally well qualified to assess the work of his contemporaries. It was not until 1968 that he scored a kind of official recognition by placing top of a critics' poll as a talent deserving of wider acclaim, but those who *know* had been spreading the good word for years. Blue Note Records are protectors of the jazz status quo and that he turns up on three out of four dates for the label proves how often his skills are demanded for playing orthodox jazz, but he is equally at home in the avant garde milieu. The difference between Billy and some of the other free percussionists is that he knows how to keep time first and foremost, and he also knows how to make love. Bearing in mind the classic Ellington observation that " a drum is a woman ", Billy realises that once you've reached a climax, you don't try to sustain the orgasm to the point of angry retaliation.

Born in Texas in 1936 and raised in the notorious Los Angeles ghetto of Watts, Billy Higgins has been playing professionally since the age of twelve. He has spent the best part of his life listening to other drummers, observing their strengths and their weaknesses, absorbing pointers on technique and dynamics, and he could, if he so desired, also claim to be among the very first of the " free " percussionists. In the late 'fifties when no other drummer would even attempt to follow the unorthodox way that Ornette Coleman was wending, both Billy and his New Orleans-born mentor, Edward Blackwell, spent many days and nights just playing with the alto saxophonist and ingesting his revolutionary conception. " It took me a time to get used to him," Billy admitted. " But after a while I figured there ain't nobody here I'm not supposed to play *with* or make *some* kind of music with! "

As A. B. Spellman has remarked in his penetrating study of unorthodox jazz makers, it was Blackwell who taught Higgins the responsibility of the drummer and the importance of technique. " With Blackwell's technique and with his knowledge of the sonics of drums, he was able to play overtones that few drummers were aware of, and this knowledge he imparted to Higgins."* Thus, when Blackwell returned to New Orleans just prior to Coleman's recording début, his pupil was his obvious replacement. Higgins appeared on three of Coleman's classic 1959 dates, his extreme looseness notably complementing the leader's aggressive spontaneity.

A modest man, Billy prefers to lay the freedom honours at the feet of the indefatigable Roy Haynes. " Cats aren't hip to Roy because he was with Sarah [Vaughan] at the time the role of the drums was developing," he said. " But as far as dexterity is concerned, Roy was playing *then* what Elvin [Jones] and Tony [Williams] are playing now. He didn't go completely wild; he still kept the taste. He kept everything in context because the drums, after all, are the navigator of the whole thing."

His own approach to the drums affords a lesson both in navigation and in lovemaking for those who really listen. Whether he is working with Coleman — he has briefly revisited his old stomping ground after an absence of some years — or with more conventional units led by such as Jackie McLean, Art Farmer, Lee Morgan or Hank Mobley, Billy exhibits taste at all times and a high degree of thoughtful consideration for the soloist. He cooks continually but knows how to save up his explosions, and in so doing he resembles

* *Four Lives in the Bebop Business*, A. B. Spellman. MacGibbon & Kee, London, 1968.

another of the great originals of percussion. Speaking of Art Blakey, Billy said, "As strong as he plays, he always starts down there with the shading. It's something that comes with age."

He also knows that the drums are the easiest of instruments to overplay and that the key to successful and sensitive percussion lies in being able to hear every instrument on the bandstand at any given time. "Even the real powerful horn players like Sonny Rollins listen to the bass all the time, so, you're not supposed to drown it out. Kenny Clarke is the master as far as drums are concerned. He really turned me on for sound. He can play like the wind!"

When Billy was a child, his closest friend, Johnny Kirkwood, was a drummer. His own family was musical, too, and as a result of this environment he soon started to play the drums himself. "I got my feelings out on playing drums more than anything else," was how he explained the attraction the music had for him. His first real jazz engagement took him on the road with the Jazz Messiahs, a band co-led by trumpeter Don Cherry and alto saxophonist George Newman, both early Ornette Coleman associates also. It was, in fact, in Newman's garage that the drummer later met Edward Blackwell, and started rehearsing with Ornette.

Prior to that, his work had been confined to the usual round of funky but musically mundane rhythm-and-blues groups. Billy paid his dues backing such singers as Amos Milburn and Bo Diddley, and it was while working with Jimmy Witherspoon that he first ran into Ornette Coleman. "You'd think it was quite a contrast and it was," he commented. "But then in a way it's not. Ornette has sure got a lot of blues in him, you see, and he's a very soulful cat. He'd swing you into bad health just from the way he plays!"

At the time Billy started his professional career, rhythm-and-blues was the only medium of self-expression available to the creative young musician. "To have a jazz gig then you really had to be into something," he said, comparing the situation to the overnight leadership demanded by some of today's young musicians. "Younger cats nowadays just seem to start playing and the first thing they hop on is jazz. In those days you had to play R&B and shows and things, but it did something for you; it was all music. That was the only way, unless you had a big name, and then the only cats who had their own bands were those who came out of Billy Eckstine's thing and such." He was referring to Miles Davis, Gene Ammons, Dexter Gordon, Art Blakey and the many other " name " musicians who swelled the phenomenal lineup of the singer's fabled 1944–47 big band.

In the late 'forties and early 'fifties, Billy worked at various times with saxophonists James Clay, Teddy Edwards, Walter Benton and Dexter Gordon. He also appeared with groups led by bassist Leroy Vinnegar and the late pianist Carl Perkins, but the real turnaround in his musical thinking came when he met Ornette Coleman. All his other associates were well-respected, hard-hitting beboppers, and Coleman was a definite outsider. Nevertheless, his originality and the spark that illuminated his vital music made an impact that Billy was unable to ignore. " It's a funny thing," the drummer mused, " but it's that spark that does it. It's the thing that really opens up people's feelings."

More than anything, he considered his association with the saxophonist as a kind of challenge because Coleman was constantly being rejected. " Cats wouldn't even dig being around him," laughed the drummer. " When he started playing, they figured, ' Well, if that's what's happening, where am I? ' But I dug that he loved music so much, and he was so serious that I took to him right away. . . ."

The general acceptance and the acclaim now paid to Ornette Coleman not only by the jazz establishment but by such non-jazz figures as Leonard Bernstein speak volumes for Billy Higgins's degree of perception. He was fortunate indeed to be endowed with such far-sightedness and sensitivity, especially in view of the attitudes of the majority of Los Angeles musicians. He has vivid recollections of those who would gather around Ornette just to sneer at his unconventional disregard of set tempos, keys and chords. " Man, I dig *you*, but I don't know what the hell *he's* doing " was one of the least caustic comments hurled at Billy by the local faces. " And Ornette would be playing his heart out! I wasn't looking at it technically, I was just thinking in terms of my feelings," he said simply.

Billy Higgins's perception stems from having a wide-open mind. " A lot of people make this mistake about music," he explained. " If a cat figures he *knows* music, his mind is closed. He figures it has to be *this* way or it has to be *that* way, and so it stops him from really enjoying it. To dig someone like Ornette you've really got to open your mind and your heart and really *listen* to him. That's the only way you'll get to him. It's a funny thing, but I've seen cats get mad with Ornette, really mad, and they say, ' Oh, man, what *is* that cat playing? ' And then they'll listen. And then they'd be right back there the next night, sitting in the same place at the bar, listening again ! "

A knowing grin mixed up his mobile face and he laughed. " Being able to open your heart to music, I figure you can learn from almost anybody, especially if that person is an *individual*. There are so few of those in jazz today; you can't have all chiefs and no Indians, you know. But the more individuals you have, the faster jazz progresses."

When Billy first started " woodshedding ", or working out ideas, with Ornette, he attempted to concentrate on overall sound effects rather than become too involved with the actual mechanics of the drums. This was a method developed by Edward Blackwell, the young man's close friend and eternal inspiration. " I wasn't thinking of the drums as drums as much as of how I could get something out of the music," he said. " That's why the way Ornette was playing helped me out, too." He also cited the bassist Leroy Vinnegar as a tower of strength : " He was one of the first cats I played with who played so *even*. The way their conception was at the time, I figured that anything I played would be cool. They [Coleman and Vinnegar] were just so strong that whatever I'd play would be no hassle. It would be just like sitting there and letting the drums play themselves."

When Atlantic Records' artists-and-repertoire man Nesuhi Ertegun heard Coleman in Los Angeles and brought him east to record, Billy Higgins with trumpeter Don Cherry and the resilient bassist Charlie Haden made the trip, too. He stayed with the saxophonist for two years which included a year at the Five Spot in New York City, but prior to making the trip east, work had been virtually non-existent for the quartet.

" During that time we had maybe one gig," Billy recalled, but without any bitterness on show. " Whatever has happened to Ornette since then he really deserved. He really was ninety per cent saxophone and ten per cent sleep. He opened up my mind because, as far as conventional playing is concerned, everything just comes down to four-, eight-, sixteen- or thirty-two-bar phrases. He started writing things that were eleven bars or six. If you listen to it, it's natural, too, but it kind of made you think another way. And there was no restriction, and since thirty-two bars had me hung up for a long time, I enjoyed that."

On the subject of greater freedom for the percussionist, Billy returned to the most versatile of jazz drummers, Roy Haynes, whose taste has few equals. " When most of the cats were playing that strict 4/4 feeling, Roy was spreading the rhythm out. The steady cymbal beat is kind of restrictive to horn players so that when they get ready to play, you hear nothing but eighth-notes.

" I used to play with Slim Gaillard a long time ago, and he showed me a lot, like hand-claps and so on. As far as the cymbals are concerned, the ride cymbal on the top is very important. That more or less sustains the rhythm, so if you play different rhythms on the top, the horn player is more or less freed to the point where, if he wants to play something on the downbeat or the upbeat, it's no hassle because you can turn the beat around very easily."

To illustrate the reverse, he recalled a night when Arthur Taylor, one of the tastiest workmen from the rhythmically more conventional era, sat in with Ornette. " He plays real hard on the sock cymbal, you see, and the next thing you know, Ornette had played something, the beat had turned around backwards, and Art couldn't get back to where it was originally at ! That showed me right there that you have to stretch the beat out to where it's not continual. For me, playing otherwise now would be kind of frustrating."

One of the distinctive aspects of a certain school of contemporary jazz percussion is the setting up of pulsating layers of sound that leave little room for the spaces and pauses inherent in the work of drummers who followed the earlier patterns. Billy maintains, " You've got to know when *not* to play ", and he pointed to Thelonious Monk's playing as an object lesson in the use of silence. " Monk can really hip a drummer to that, if he listens to him. He is a school within himself, and in the little time I worked with him, I really learned a lot."

He used Monk's magisterial dominance as a comparison with the authoritativeness of his favourite leader. " Ornette plays like Thelonious or Coleman Hawkins, he's that calibre of musician. He makes a lot of demands on you. I've seen cats get mad with him, and I've seen him make them disgusted with themselves. He's an awful strong person." The drummer, who has the ability to play in any style, puts Ornette on a different level to those who, he said, have misunderstood the meaning of " freedom " and translated it into anarchy. " I can dig all kinds of music as long as it's pure, but a lot of cats made freedom an excuse. Ornette really turned a lot of cats around, but some of them turned too much ! A lot of them took to playing like that, but you've got to take it in doses. You can't just throw it all out there.

" I've played with Ornette when he's turned around and said, ' Let's play " Sophisticated Lady " ', and he's done just that. But some cats wouldn't believe it if they saw it. Also, he has that thing that Bird had of playing so much *rhythm*. He's so much brighter, so much livelier than anyone else. I get the feeling of Coleman Hawkins or Sonny Rollins played at 45 rpm, because Ornette can really play with that spark."

Billy cited Tony Williams and Frank Butler as two of his favourite drummers, together with Edward Blackwell, Roy Haynes and Elvin Jones. " And there's an older cat in St Louis called Joe Charles. He can really play. He works on a fish truck most of the time, but he can really play his heart out." He went on to bewail the lack of what he calls individuality in the percussion field today. " It's very seldom that you can hear a drummer today and say, ' That's So-and-so.' I guess it's like it was with the alto saxophone and Charlie Parker. First off, everyone's trying to sound like Philly Joe

Jones. Next thing, everyone's trying to sound like Elvin. Most of the cats are trying to get into that bag, but we really need more originality. I see certain possibilities, but not that many. Maybe Lenny McBrowne; he's nice."

The drummer pointed out that there used to be an abundance of good, accomplished percussion men but that now such selfless perennials are at a premium and greatly in demand. One reason for this, he suggested, is that the majority of drummers are so involved in self-expression that they have little or no interest in absorbing the concept of the leader. "You can't always do it the way *you* want to, you have to play *their* music, too. Now, everybody wants to be out front, but the drummer's supposed to give a little and take a little and give a little and so on. When you're not a star, there's a lot of pressure off you and you can just be yourself. Sometimes I've seen people who've become stars, and it's all over for them."

Billy is no star in the accepted sense of the word, yet in a world where it's every man for himself, his good-natured adaptability and thoughtful flavouring make him a shining beacon of achievement. An original drummer with a never diminishing love for the music itself, he is one of an apparently diminishing breed of musicians who live for jazz. You don't often see his ideas and opinions in the jazz magazines, for he is not one of the incessantly roaring soapbox orators spawned by the new music and the concurrent social upheaval; his credo is live and let live. The music, too, is his life, and he has scant respect for musicians who attempt to claim any particular mode of expression as their personal property.

He has the old-time musicians' habit of underlining his words as he speaks, but the stress was especially pronounced when he stated, "Music don't *belong* to *nobody*. If they could just realise that music doesn't come *from* you, it comes *through* you, and if you don't get the right vibrations, you might kill a little bit of it. You can't take music for granted."

He is an emotional player himself and so he holds in the highest esteem those musicians, great or small, who have the ability to move the listener. "What makes jazz jazz is often the people who don't know anything about it," he said. "The kind of people who, if a quarter-note was to walk in the door would think it was a wine bottle. But they'd make you *cry*. And if things like that can happen for someone who knows nothing about music at all, then naturally you know there's got to be something happening with this music.

"Wilbur Ware used to make everybody shut up. People would be clinking their glasses and so on, but he would start playing, and you'd hear that magic. You could hear a pin drop in the house. To communicate with people, you have to have it born in you."

Billy has some of that magic, too, and it's something that stems from knowing about love. When I met him in New York he was far from fit and swollen hands were making playing difficult for him. Rumours were flying that he was undependable and yet he continued to show up for even poorly-paid club dates. "It's a funny thing," mused one leader after a successful Sunday matinée. "I really didn't think Billy would make it today, but he did and he played so *good* it was a gas to have him there. I guess the thing is that he really loves music so much."

And that is the little drummer man's secret. While so many of the young Turks wrestle with their vituperative horns and spend most of their non-playing time talking about "communication", Billy Higgins is out there getting on with the job. He knows, you see, and he communicates without stopping to think about it. It's something born in him.

Chapter Six

A policy of non-compromise

If you don't have the whole spiritual thing, I don't think
jazz is complete. . . . If I can't communicate, I don't care
how hip the music is supposed to be, how avant garde, how
square or whatever, I don't think it's worth producing.

JIMMY HEATH

A policy of non-compromise

Jazz has done pretty well for itself considering its background and origins. Born in the brothels of New Orleans and shunted through school in the Chicago, New York and Kansas City underworld, it now finds itself regarded as an art form, although its acceptance as such is still as fraught with condescension as is white America's approbation of the Negro as citizen. But, even within the ghetto, jazz as a way of life carries with it the stamp of progressiveness.

But that's about as far as it goes. Many musicians are conservative in their sociological and cultural outlook, especially in their attitudes towards the inevitable musical revolution. Although it is often said that the style of a master transcends categories and makes conscious efforts to move with the times unnecessary, every aware musician knows that as each decade passes, he is one step further from contemporaneity. Occasionally, as in the case of tenor saxophonist Sonny Rollins, he will be able to embrace new developments wholeheartedly and assimilate them into his existing concept without sacrificing his artistry, but more often than not to do so is interpreted as leaping self-consciously onto the bandwagon. Most musicians prefer to stay with the music they know, adding the merest hint of up-to-date flavouring. Such a man is Jimmy Heath.

A small, cool, self-contained man who seldom allows a smile to awaken his cynical, hooded eyes, Jimmy is the middle brother in a noted family of musical Philadelphians. Three years younger than Percy, the aloof bassist with the Modern Jazz Quartet, and nine years older than drummer Albert, his essentially masculine tenor saxophone style is firmly entrenched in the mainstream of jazz. The list of men with whom he has shared the bandstand reads like a jazz Who's Who of the past two decades. He is typical of the musician who has developed his playing to the point where he still seeks to improve it but without altering direction, and even if his sound does carry superficially contemporary overtones, he has few kind words for the new movement in general. A conservative, yes, but one who has proved his worth.

It was a sticky, stifling, New York summer's afternoon when Jimmy came by to talk about music; the kind of day for relaxing and drinking beer, but he was brimming over with words. " The music business needed a shot in the arm from the avant garde to give it a lift and the flavour of excitement that it had lost," he declared initially. " Other than that lift, the mainstream is still very valid to me. I think that there are a lot of people who will get back to that when this frustrated, wild age is over." Even within the mainstream itself, he added, there are only a handful of players with anything new to say. " It's the same with the avant garde; there are a lot of impostors and rejects in that movement."

Several of the saxophonist's formative years were spent in close proximity to the late John Coltrane — " a twenty-year friend of mine from the time he came to Philadelphia from Hamlet, North Carolina " — and he understandably resents those he describes as " carbon copies of John " who have sprung up in the titan's wake. His eyebrows arched mirthlessly : " It seems like everybody is trying to be like his twin or something. You go into any little city around the United States, and I know it's the same in Europe, and everybody is playing like Coltrane. This is very bad for the music because there is no originality like there used to be."

Coltrane was studying music in Philadelphia when he and Jimmy first met and both of them were playing alto saxophone. They both later switched to tenor at more or less the same time and became, together with Benny Golson, the leading hip young locals on the instrument. " At that time there were so many different tenor players I could identify just by listening to them. If you listened to the radio and Gene Ammons came on, you knew Gene Ammons. If Dexter Gordon came on, you knew right away. You knew Lucky Thompson, Don Byas, Lester Young, Coleman Hawkins and Ben Webster; they all had their own identity."

Jimmy conceded that when he and Coltrane were working in Dizzy Gillespie's big band around 1950, their model and

Golson's was Dexter Gordon. " He was like the advanced Lester Young with his chords and things, and everybody leaned on him a little at the time, including guys like Sonny Stitt when he was playing tenor. But after you've been doing things for some time you begin to find something of your own out of music. I don't think you can always find it right away, it takes time, but Coltrane was one who had an originality at the time when everybody else seemed to be leaning on other people."

Jimmy was, and is, perturbed at the disproportionate degree of attention focused on some of Coltrane's disciples even during the late saxophonist's lifetime, attention he considers totally unwarranted in view of the followers' lack of originality. " I remember one time in Philadelphia when John was playing at the Showboat and Charles Lloyd was just up the road at Pep's with Cannonball," he recalled. " People kept telling me, ' Man, how d'you like this Charles Lloyd? ' and I was saying, ' Why don't you go around the corner and hear the original? ' "

He shook his head sadly. " People just like Lloyd's image, you see — not that I take anything from his musicianship. He's a good musician, but in the United States, in fact in New York alone, I could find fifteen or twenty tenor players who, with the right publicity, the right backing and the right record exposure, could be another Charles Lloyd or even greater."

Jimmy Heath's stringent comments were made relatively objectively and without rancour, although his attitude could easily be misconstrued. Lloyd's name and his bush of shaggy hair are well known to the public that follows modern popular music in both Europe and America, whereas Jimmy has no " name " value to speak of. He is lucky to be referred to as " the brother of the bassist with the MJQ ", and so he speaks with feeling. He is one of the consistent bastions of non-compromise whom time and changing styles have sadly cheated of recognition by all save other musicians.

He does not seek to detract from the undoubted musicianship of a man like Lloyd, nor to comment sourly on the fame that has eluded him; but he hits on the inescapable fact that musicians now need an " image " in order to reach the public. Pianist Herbie Nicholls once said, " It seems like you either have to be an Uncle Tom or a drug addict to make it in jazz ",* and nowadays it's the shot-silk kaftans, the beads and the hair that make the impact, as often as the music. When Charles Lloyd shakes his marraccas ineffectively at the audience, contorting his lanky body in caricature of the defiant Mick Jagger, it looks like he's really into something. Jimmy Heath dresses soberly in charcoal-grey or dark blue suits and so his applause is confined to the jazz people who *know*. But for them his own wholesome saxophone style is far more viable than Lloyd's titillating eclecticism.

Jimmy Heath's words revealed a state of affairs where, if the artist is neither extrovert nor opportunist, the chances for exposure can easily pass him at the speed of sound. Publicity is necessary today and that, he claimed, is something that comes about only through good timing. " Someone like Lloyd has gotten considerable help from the Press, but it's probably just because he was in the right place at the right time when somebody came in who could help him. On the other hand, if he wasn't exposed, he could not solicit publicity, either, or get any help from those who could give him a push."

The saxophonist has recently adapted his own playing to assimilate a taste of today, yet in spite of his incessant thirst for improvisation he seems doomed to remain a " musicians' musician ". Although few such artists ever escape from that category, Jimmy himself considers that a good recording contract would help his name to reach a wider public. Among musicians his reputation as a writer equals his reputation as a saxophonist, and back in the old days when the Riverside label gave record dates to all the good, consistent musicians of his generation, Jimmy was number one man for co-owner Orrin Keepnews. He wrote arrangements for nearly every session, contributed tunes and made half a dozen albums under his own name. " That relationship spoiled me, I guess. Orrin Keepnews was the type of person who would seek you out. You don't get those kind of people in the business today."

---

* *Four Lives in the Bebop Business*, by A. B. Spellman. MacGibbon & Kee, London, 1968.

Since then he has been offered a contract by one company whose policy was alien to his own, " of the type that limits you. They just want you to sit up and blow with a quartet." For Jimmy, free-for-all jam sessions belong in the past; he favours carefully thought out music and so he rejected the offer.

He admits to feeling discouraged occasionally when he picks up the music papers and sees the names of Charles Lloyd and Archie Shepp staring at him week after week, yet he knows on the other hand that for most of his life he has managed to maintain his family through music alone without compromising his artistic standards. He has taken rock-and-roll gigs when he had a narcotic habit to support, but he has kept his respect for the music in which he believes. " Money," he said sagely, " is not the problem for me. When you've played with everybody from Miles on down it speaks for itself."

His sights are set on an annually increasing income of modest proportions. " I don't see any big rush to get rich. Just to be contented and happy is more important, but in some places it takes a lot of money to do that! I know there are some musicians whose agents get them articles in *Time* or *Esquire* and all that, and it's good for them if they make it that way, but if I don't make it through playing, I just don't make it. A lot of groups get financial backing, make a big splash and then die away. I prefer to make mine by music and if I can't do that, then I'd rather not have it."

In spite of protestations to the contrary, the younger musicians tend to be more publicity-conscious than those of Jimmy Heath's generation. Even among the militants who act as though the journalists (i.e. the white power structure) owe them a living, requests for interviews are rarely turned down and appointments are usually kept. " Are you paying me for this? " they will often ask the representatives of low-budget jazz magazines in all seriousness and then, when their gambit fails, relax the pugnacious exterior and talk long and loud about sincerity and soul. Jimmy's words reflect an older, less-complicated way of life but a none the less proud and self-reliant attitude.

" You see, I'm not the sort of person to go up to somebody

and say, ' I would like to record for your record company ', and write up a whole brochure of all the things I have done for the past twenty-five years. I'll never start making tapes to take along for people to hear me, I'll just continue to live like I'm living. If you come down and hear me play, you'll find the reason why I haven't been no overnight success."

At the time of this interview, Jimmy was featured sideman with a mellifluous quintet led by the lyrical fluegelhornist Art Farmer. That combo has since broken up, yet his comments about the partnership reveal his personal musical inclinations. " I'd been waiting for a leader who has the ability to be a good leader without a whole lot of personal problems. I could be a leader but I don't need all the problems that go with the leadership. Art is not only a good leader himself but a very good player, and I really respect his melodic concept because basically I'm a melodic soloist, too. This way, he has left me plenty of room."

Jimmy also leads his own group from time to time and makes all vibraharpist Milt Jackson's dates away from the confines of the Modern Jazz Quartet. Melodic interest dominates in these units and so it is not surprising to learn that the saxophonist finds most avant garde music so " harsh " and " violent " that he is unable to accept it from a musical standpoint. " As long as the music has a sense of humour and a little love, it's OK," he stipulated. " I like ballads and I've gotten maybe my warmest response and reaction from playing them sometimes. I'm like Art Farmer and Milt Jackson where that's concerned.

" First and foremost, I like melodies, and so I can enjoy Ornette Coleman's compositions and his playing of the saxophone. He is definitely a leader and so is Don Cherry, another unsung hero of the avant garde. His compositions are beautiful. As a writer Don says something, but as a trumpeter it's hard to get past his poor tone quality. When a tone is not quite pleasing, that leads to problems of communication."

Jimmy's technique has improved considerably in the last few years since he freed himself from the strictures of drug addiction and has more leisure time in which to concentrate on music. He practises flute assiduously and is, he says, " getting a better idea of breathing ". The firm grounding he gained by working in the Dizzy Gillespie big band of 1950–51 and with such luminaries as trumpeters Howard McGhee and Kenny Dorham and trombonist J. J. Johnson is reflected in his unhurried way of getting on with the music without any fuss. Longer lines figure more now in his playing than the accented bebop style but that is the extent of his " modernity ".

From the plethora of younger tenor saxophonists invading the scene, he singles out the mature approach of Wayne Shorter and Joe Henderson for his admiration. Like himself, they are well rooted in orthodoxy, even if their concept is a trifle more progressive than his own. " I think we have a little more taste for employing these new, different styles than some people who are just starting out playing music," he said, stressing the importance of background. " There was a guy who told me that one day there would come a time when you could get a saxophone in the morning and make a job that night. The way some people play, I think it may have happened already ! "

When work is sparse, Jimmy's worries are few. He has fifty or so royalty-earning compositions out, among them the modern jazz standards " Gemini " and " Big P ", written for brother Percy. " My advantage," he said, " is in being a writer. When the jazz gigs don't come through I can always sit home and think up a tune to give to one of my friends who like my music. I've just written two new ones for Cannonball Adderley and Miles [Davis] is always asking me to bring in some more music. I also write for Herbie Mann and when people like that record an album that sells twenty or thirty thousand copies, that's a nice little taste to come in out of the mails when you're not working ! "

So, little known though he may be, Jimmy Heath keeps busy while maintaining his policy of non-compromise. " I'm not at all depressed because I don't have the stature that other people have — these things will come," he said philosophically. " I know one thing : if you understand what you're doing and you are convincing enough, then the people will understand what you're doing, regardless."

This diminutive man is a firm believer in communication with the audience. He is not interested in attaining the kind of respectability that the concert platform stands for if he cannot move the people. " If you don't have the whole spiritual thing, I don't think jazz is complete. To me, a musician is just a transformer. It's like I receive the music from somewhere else. If I sit down to write a tune, nobody comes up and tells me what to write, it comes from somewhere else. It's not really mine, I'm supposed to transform this music. If I can't communicate, I don't care how hip the music is supposed to be, how avant garde, how square or whatever, I don't think it's worth producing."

Although Jimmy Heath may be some way from gianthood in a profession packed with minor talents, there is little he produces that is not worthwhile. " I've never heard Jimmy play a bad night," Art Farmer once said admiringly, and anyone who has followed his career over the years will testify to that. Jimmy doesn't believe in coasting, his policy is to get out front and get on with the music. In 1966 his fortieth birthday passed by calmly and without any fuss. " Life begins at forty," he said with a smile, and in terms of his wider acceptance the uncompromising son of Philadelphia intends to see that it does.

Chapter Seven

Back to the African heartbeat

The heart is the first instrument that man became aware of, and I'm sure that's how the drum came to be. It is as old as civilisation itself and if you look around you, you'll realise that the whole world is based on rhythm.

RANDY WESTON

Back to the African heartbeat

Morocco has always offered a kind of haven for the traveller who wants to escape from the Western way of life without actually going too far afield. It's a country with the quality of timelessness, a land bursting with a feast of smells, colours and sounds that go easy on the eye and ear and senses. Cultural contrasts abound there, too, and from a racial point of view the climate is healthily heterogeneous. There is plenty of poverty there and religious restrictions, but for a black American who feels his entire life has been spent at the focal point of hostile eyes, the freedom Morocco can offer is like the realisation of a dream.

As far back as the 'twenties the American jazz fraternity began to lose some of its members to the beguiling charms of the freer European existence and in the last ten years the number of Americans-in-residence abroad has grown astronomically. Randy Weston went one better. With the impulsive do-or-die philosophy that has coloured his entire life, he did what the other cats only talked about and moved back to Africa.

Heads still turn when the dignified ebony-coloured pianist walks through Rabat's crumbling old Medina or toils up a twisting Tangier hillside, but for the first time in forty years he can be reassured by the fact that he stands over six-foot-seven and is quite a memorable sight.

"The main thing here is that you make it on your own merit," was his comment after nearly a year away from home. "Nobody is impressed if you're blond or black; they may be impressed if you're six-foot-seven but that can happen anywhere. It's true that there is a heavy class system in Africa, but in everyday things, what you can do matters more than your background."

Recently, Randy decided that he had gone just as far as he could in the insecure American jazz world, and for a man with three children to support, that may not be very far. Unless you have the good fortune to be a Louis Armstrong or a Duke Ellington, the critics will lavish praise on your music while your pockets stay unreassuringly empty. What's more, the audience for jazz in America is dying by the hour and Randy, who has been living in Morocco since January 1968, feels he escaped while the going was good.

" If you ask me how I feel about being away from the mainstream of jazz, all I can say is that I was away from it in New York," he said, carefully considering his self-imposed exile. " Musicians tend to play just what they feel but the writers give labels to the music so that the new thing tends to push the older thing out of the limelight. But as for the so-called New Thing in New York, I found it was gradually making me angrier and angrier about the situation in modern-day life.

" So I haven't really missed anything, because when I was in the States I stayed in my own little cave and listened to the music I liked. I was still as amazed by Ellington when I left as I was ten years ago."

Randy Weston is one of those superlative musicians who always found work but never quite made it financially or in terms of attracting a wider public. His highly percussive style stems primarily from his actual size and his love of the drums, and is heavily influenced by what he calls the " Duke–Monk school ". Earl Hines, likewise a powerful two-fisted man at the keyboard, was another potent inspiration, and Randy takes pride in hearing his name coupled with these three piano giants. " I've always been heavily influenced by people who played strong," he admitted, " and by becoming more aware of African music, too, in many senses I use the piano as a more percussive instrument. I will get actual drum effects on it, too."

He is also a composer of delightful melodies — " Little Niles ", " Pam's Waltz " and " Hi-Fly " are just three out of almost a hundred memorable pieces — and he plays with a dynamic rhythmic attack that has rarely been equalled in jazz piano. In short, he is one of the most under-rated of the under-rated musicians and, because he arrived comparatively late on the scene and then chose to lead his own trios and quartets rather than work as a sideman with a famous leader, he is one of the music's unsung heroes.

In the immediate postwar years his father owned four luncheonettes in Brooklyn. One of them, Frank's, was not only an afterhours hangout for the local musicians but a place that attracted all the major figures in bebop. Dizzy Gillespie, Leo Parker, Bud Powell, Miles Davis and Max Roach were regular patrons and Randy made sure that good music and conversation were on the menu, too. " We had the hippest jukebox anywhere in New York," he recalled. " Cats would finish a gig in Manhattan and take the subway down for a cup of coffee and a hamburger. We had Stravinsky and Bird on that jukebox, man, and the conversation was heavy every night."

Roach was a Brooklynite, too, and the musicians would congregate at his apartment after leaving the restaurant. It was there that Randy met Charlie Parker and played with him in the atmosphere of easy camaraderie that used to exist in those days. He recalled his trepidation when he first met the alto saxophonist. " Max said, ' Hey, Randy, play a number for Bird ', and I was nervous to play — as great as this cat was! I said to myself, what could I play that would interest him? But I played and he was knocked out. He said, ' Man, you're gonna play; you keep on playing and you'll be a good musician.' "

Randy was still involved in the restaurant business but he had become accepted by the Brooklyn clique as a fine pianist in his own right. When he finally made up his mind that music was *it*, his first jazz gigs were with groups led by the fiery drummer Art Blakey, alto saxophonist Eddie (Cleanhead) Vinson and trumpeter Kenny Dorham; then he joined forces with an old neighbourhood compadre, the baritone saxophonist Cecil Payne. He was the first artist to record for the now defunct Riverside label in 1955, the same year that he scored a New Star award in the *Down Beat* poll and started to achieve recognition as a composer, too.

For a while he had a plain and functional house furnished in the sparse but welcoming Moroccan style in the capital,

Rabat; now he and his son live in Tangier. It's a far cry
from the bubbling restlessness of Brooklyn. Randy plans eventually to tour the African continent and record the rapidly
diminishing indigenous folklore. In the meantime all his
interests are focused on Morocco. Already the clamour of the
North African market place can be heard in his music, and
the haunting sound of Berber flute music that lies midway
between bagpipes and the blues colours his earthy compositions. Such new pieces as "Marrakesh Blues" and "A Night
In The Medina" are so evocative of their unique and ancient
sources of inspiration that you can almost smell the charcoal,
cous-cous, leather and *kif* that pungently vie with each other
in the local atmosphere.

In Morocco the pianist has found surprising enthusiasm for
his own music, too. Whether he dons a dress-suit to play piano
before a concert audience in Tangier or rolls up his shirt
sleeves for an impromptu percussion session among villagers in
the secretive Rif mountains, he commands interest and respect
from local musicians. He can sit down and hold a mutually
amusing conversation in sign-language with dancers like Bou-
chara, omnipotent queen of the Goulimines, the indigo-stained
"blue people" who live at the edge of the Sahara; and all
this he has done with jazz, a kind of music which the theorists
claim is totally alien to the country's culture. Randy has proved
that the beat is universal.

Not only does he leave joyous hearts behind him wherever
he plays, but the debonair pianist has also started to make
concrete cultural contributions by lecturing extensively about
jazz and the influence that African and Arabic music has had
on his own writing. During a concert he always demonstrates
how a particular work has grown from a simple melodic or
rhythmic pattern remembered from the daily abundance of
sound that beats on the ear in Africa, and although he stipulates that he has no set method when it comes to writing,
Randy is forever conscious of rhythm.

" I've been this way since the late 'fifties when I first started
to write, but here in Africa the feeling is stronger. If I hear
a rhythm that appeals to me, I'll go to the piano, take that
rhythm, and from it I'll create a melody. Although there are

times when I get melodic ideas, usually the tune follows the rhythm I have in my head. I try to keep my antennae open to be aware of other kinds of music and just the sounds of life, like the rhythm of a horsecart or the sound of somebody whistling, for the sounds of nature alone can inspire a composition."

In Africa where the sounds of nature predominate, Randy has come to consider them more complex than the roar of the big city. "Ellington used the sounds of the city in his writing, but whatever he does, you can always hear the blues," he explained. "And I think that so-called blues feeling, both its rhythm and its sound, is the sound of the African village."

Back in 1966, when the pianist visited Gabon as part of a U.S. State Department tour, he had first-hand experience of how the music imitates the vibrations of African life. "I attended a very interesting ceremony where all kinds of music, both Catholic and tribal, were played. Then I went into the forest with my tape-recorder. I simply recorded the sound of the insects and the wind and the birds at night, but it was fantastic. It was like a complete orchestra of counter-rhythms. It was as though each member of the forest had its own little rhythm, and somehow I noticed this all over Africa — especially with the people — everyone has their own rhythm going. You can see from this that the music and the natural surroundings of Africa are related."

When I asked Randy to pose for a photograph playing on an unfamiliar drum and surrounded by curious villagers, he flatly refused. "I have too much respect for the drum and for African music to fool with it," he said, although he later capitulated when an impromptu session arose out of our visit. Yet his refusal to be photographed under staged conditions was typical of this strong-willed man who lives as close to the heartbeat of Africa as he can. He is almost religious in his fervour for things African and is continually affirming his love for the drum, the instrument that, he says, "echoes the heartbeat".

He is a great man for theories, but there is one in particular that he is always repeating. "The heart is the first instrument that man became aware of, and I'm sure that's how the drum came to be. It is as old as civilisation itself and if you look around you, you'll realise that the whole world is based on rhythm."

Rhythm, of course, is the keynote of jazz, and the African continent is packed to the edges with its varied and good vibrations. Randy's statement uncannily echoed what another pianist, South Africa's Dollar Brand, once told me : " The whole of Africa moves in time to music. We sow seeds to music and we sing songs to the corn to make it grow and to the sky to make it rain. Then we reap our harvest to the sound of music and song."

The late Edmond Hall, a unique New Orleans clarinettist, made an abortive attempt, which lasted a couple of years, to settle in Ghana, yet with the exception of the indefatigable Louis Armstrong and Lionel Hampton, the man who made the vibraharp come of age, few other jazzmen have taken the logical trip back to the birthplace of rhythm. Randy Weston had been there seven times before he decided to take a chance and stay, and now he feels at home there, literally, and that is the key to his happiness. He still clings to a vestige of bourgeois American " respectability " by wearing mohair trousers and keeping his hair trimmed, but sometimes he'll be seen sporting a beautiful Ghanaian *batakari* — a gift from admirers there — and looking good in it. At home he and his son Niles wear personal variations on the flowing West African robe that the Yorubas call *agbada* and Randy lets his massive feet relax in a pair of bright yellow Moroccan slippers. In Tangier his family and friends sup from heavy earthenware dishes and more often than not the cuisine is local. The life suits the easy-going pianist; his own personal warmth is ideally complemented by the tropical heat and the tantalisingly spicy food.

When he walks through the streets, greeting friends in his limited but functional Arabic, his walk is sometimes juttingly American, sometimes totally African as he lopes along and rolls back on his heels. " It's gotten so that I can look African whenever I want," he smiled with a mixture of amusement and pride. " Some people think I'm from Senegal; they never think I'm American till I open my mouth ! "

An amiable, open-minded and personable giant of a man, Randy has a capacity for understanding Africa and its people and being understood in return that stems from nothing more than sincerity and a gregarious nature. In this he is again exceptional, for in the past many black Americans who visited the continent of their ancestors' origin looked for a kind of Canaan but left, finding nothing. Notable among the disillusioned was the novelist Richard Wright, who reported that he found no love there. Randy has a different story to tell.

" I think that if one lives in Africa one has to have a basic love for nature and for life, just for the more natural things. It doesn't mean that one has to be poor, but even if you've got the biggest house in Africa, there's something basic about your existence. There are a lot of people who can't see this, can't adjust, but I think that here you'll find whatever you come looking for. And I've found more love here than any place I've been."

Born in Brooklyn in 1926, Randy grew up in a notoriously rough section of one of the world's most violent cities. Not surprisingly, he always regarded violence as commonplace and it was not until he went to Africa that he realised there were places without it — at least on a personal level.

" And it was such a feeling of relief," he smiled gratefully. " People are so gentle and kind here, you know, they'll go out of their way to help you. Many times I've been out on the road and someone will stop his car to help you, or stop what he's doing, put down his work and go with you. And if you're interested in their music, they'll go all out to show you what's happening."

He first encountered this spirit of musical brotherhood when he went to Nigeria in 1961. Five years later he took a sextet that featured tenor saxophonist Clifford Jordan, drummer Ed Blackwell and fluegelhornist Ray Copeland on a U.S. government-sponsored visit to fourteen African and Middle Eastern countries. This time the feeling of friendship was even more pronounced. " Driving through a village we'd hear sounds coming from somewhere so we'd stop the car," he recalled. " We'd go and look for the music and when the people realised what we wanted, they'd talk with us, bring us food and we'd end up spending hours there, just digging."

Aside from the public's drift away from his own brand of jazz, it was the absence of such brotherly love in America today that prompted Randy to leave the land of his birth. He is a highly sensitive man in spite of a defiant, tough exterior, and the ugliness, both musical and social, that characterises today's jazz scene for him was, frankly, getting him down. " I felt the beauty was draining out of my music and I looked around me to find out why," he said. " I realised that every-thing around me was ugly — the people, the situation, the political setup, everything." Where the pianist is concerned, the avant garde is synonymous with the sound of aggression and although he has no time for the actual music itself, he is quick to point out how acutely this sound echoes the contem-porary American struggle. " The dirt is coming out from under the rug and it's being heard in the music of today," was his succinct comment.

When Randy decided to pull up stakes and head for Africa, Morocco seemed hardly the logical choice for a black militant, but it had been in this country that his 1966 sextet scored their biggest audience response. The American Embassy and the local radio stations were flooded with fanmail clamouring for the piano giant's return and it was, as he says, " not a case of us choosing Morocco but Morocco choosing us ".

Randy had no reservations about settling down in North Africa, for in his mind's eye the continent takes shape as a single entity. His long-standing interest in travelling there was initially formed by his father — sometime barber, sometime restaurateur and natural philosopher — who came to New York in 1916 from Panama. " We have a lot of West Indian blood in our family, and the West Indians in America have a tremendous sense of pride," explained Randy. " My father was no exception and he always used to talk to me about Africa. He'd talk about the old civilisations of Africa and so on and I guess he did this to me because growing up in America you can have such a tremendous sense of guilt about having a brown skin or African blood. You can feel you're just an inferior person and I think my father desired to counteract this."

As a result of his father's judicious education, the pianist was encouraged to read deeply and to take an interest in the world outside America. Gradually he began to realise just how much the white world had taken from African culture in terms not only of human lives and labour but in music, speech, dress and the entire culture of " hip ". " It's really come to the point that through the rock-and-roll thing they use our language throughout the white world," he explained.

In the early 'fifties Randy met a drummer from Guinea who gave him a first-hand account of the structure of African society. " Asedela Defora was a tremendous drummer and he told me all about tribal life, about music and the drums and how beautiful the people were. He also told me I should go there. In spite of the way we'd been taught that Africa was primitive and savage and full of cannibals and so on, this guy brought me much closer to the truth. He explained how a drummer not only has to play but has to be a poet, too; how to be able to tell stories with the drums he has to have fantastic depth."

His first chance to breathe the exotic air of the African continent came when he visited Nigeria as part of a cultural exchange programme. The contingent, which included singers Nina Simone and Brock Peters and the late Langston Hughes, the poet and playwright, represented jazz through Randy, Lionel Hampton and the bassist Ahmed Abdul-Malik, and as soon as their plane landed at Lagos, the airport was flooded with light. " We got off the plane and all of a sudden we heard the sound of drums," recalled Randy. " I knew then that this was my home."

The moment of truth took on mystical proportions when a youngster ran up to the pianist from out of nowhere, grabbed his arm and looked steadfastly into his eyes. " ' Well,' he said, ' so you finally decided to come back home ! ' He said, ' You've been gone three hundred years and you finally made it — where have you been so long? ' The moment he said that, I realised that in spite of a three- or four-hundred-year gap, spiritually and rhythmically we hadn't changed at all. You can't make a culture lie down."

The very next day Randy walked all over Lagos and everywhere he went, in market places and government buildings alike, he was reminded of 125th Street, the main street of Harlem. " I saw all these faces that I knew, people I recognised, and I kept on wanting to go over and say ' Hello ' to them." Then and there the purpose of the journey was realised. The troupe had gone to Nigeria to see what links between ex-slave and indigenous African remained; Randy found that the chain had never been broken.

His almost traumatic experience when confronted with people who resembled his grandparents and the older black people he had known since childhood was, in fact, the realisation of a dream he had never mentioned before. " I've been very fortunate in life that a lot of my dreams have come true," he said. " I feel this about life : if I want something, I set the dial in a certain direction and I'll eventually get there."

In retrospect he realised that the organisers of the tour had set out to show off the westernised American Negro rather than let him give vent to his soul, and consequently the emphasis was placed on Western music rather than jazz. After the concerts, however, the musicians soon made their way to the nightclubs and hung-out with the locals in the traditional manner, but it was not until the pianist's second visit two years later that he had his first chance to actually work with African percussionists. " And I don't know how I thought of the things those cats had me playing ! It was really wild ! "

The dominant factor in Randy Weston's unequalled ability to integrate on both musical and social levels is that he feels all African music, with the possible exception of that with the stronger Arabic influence, is rhythmically geared to man's basic nature. " I don't care if you're an intellectual or an idiot, that beat's going to get to you," he maintained. " Whether or not it's complex, it hits home inside. You do more than hear it with your ears, your whole body absorbs it. Sometimes it will take you away with it, too. The trance is universal."

His lengthy sojourn in Morocco came at the end of his fourth visit there. As a result of a solo concert where he played for a distinguished gathering in company with two Berber drummers, he was invited to work the country's leading hotel chain with his bassist Bill Wood and drummer Edward Blackwell. The Government have expressed interest in plans to establish a jazz school there and are, in fact, the only African government far-sighted enough to discuss the subject with Randy. In return for the faith that the Ministry of Tourism and others have shown in his music, the pianist has assimilated huge chunks of local folklore into his spicy sounds.

It was not difficult, for his ears were already pinned back receptively. Hardly a day goes by in the old quarter of any Moroccan town or village without the sound of the flute or the beat of the drum wafting hypnotically through the air. "Everything I've heard here so far has been like a minor blues," he noted. "The Berbers take a simple blues theme and while the rhythms keep changing in the background, they sing and they dance and even make rhythmic patterns with their feet in place of a drum in some parts of the country."

Randy has three aims in his new life. Firstly, to collect folk music for posterity; secondly, to create modern versions of the music itself; and thirdly, to inspire young Africans, and Moroccans in particular, to use the traditional forms of their music and not allow it to moulder beneath an incongruous covering of imported rock-and-roll. He recalled the joy he experienced when his own percussionist, Chief Bey, achieved huge personal reactions from African audiences during their State Department tour. "These kids have rejected their indigenous heritage, the heritage of the drum, and instead they are playing rock guitars with the volume control turned up loud. It's pitiful," Randy declared, "but it's not too late. Chief Bey turned them on to their own music, and I want to do the same.

"After all, a musicologist is limited in the sense that he can only collect and notate and catalogue tapes, but we have the advantage that we can get out there and *play*."

The particular kind of communication that the American has achieved in Morocco has replaced for him the dwindling friendship of the once abundantly social New York jazz scene. Randy has no regrets about leaving the Great Society — "taking the subway and walking down Fifth Avenue are not important to me " — and for him the scene had more or less ground to a jaded halt anyway. "The comradeship you feel in Africa is something that you notice not only with the musicians but with the people, too. Here the everyday people love music so much that you feel a closeness. Because they're closer to nature, they appreciate the simple things of life which are really the most beautiful, and wherever we travelled there has been this tremendous rapport. This is just how it used to be years ago. It seems that people in the West have forgotten how to enjoy themselves."

Although the work is scarce and he has many mouths to feed, the pianist has no words for the feeling of total relaxation which he is able to indulge himself in at last. Africa, he believes, does not change the individual so much as give him a chance to be himself. " People here live *life*, you know. A lot of them don't have very much but they make it. I'd always dreamed how Africa would be and it turned out to be just how I'd expected."

Using Morocco as a base, Randy has worked down the West African coast and, whenever possible, encouraged and taught any young aspirants he has met on the way. " What we're attempting to do now is based on a dream for the future," said the pianist. " Whether we succeed or not, we are still planting a seed. If we are able to accomplish great things, this is beautiful — if we don't, we will have started something for the others."

He feels that not only is Africa a continent of great agricultural and mineral potential, but it has tremendous musical wealth to offer as well. " The whole world has their eyes on Africa today," he explained, and he feels excited to be in at the start of a new era of discovery. Randy is a big man with a big heart and a love for people and the music of the people that has little equal in the often narrow-minded world of jazz. He is more than happy to add his hand to those already on the plough, and he has every intention of living out his allotted span on African soil. " To me, this would be the greatest way for one to spend one's life," was how he put it. Whatever country he chooses or that chooses him is immaterial. " I sort of consider Africa as one place, musically. I don't see any boundary lines as far as the music side of the culture is concerned."

Superficially, at least, it might appear that the pianist has chosen the easy way out at a time when things were tough. He has traded the tensions of the burgeoning race war for the friendship and hospitality of Africa, and exchanged the sounds that were grating heavily on his ear for the drums and the music of nature itself. But his adopted life is far from easy, for there are few places for jazz musicians to work in Africa, especially on a long-term basis.

Nevertheless, peace of mind is a state that has little equal in the world today and the highly sensitive pianist could never have found it elsewhere. Walking up the beach in Tangier one day, he was pursued by cries from a group of Moroccans who knew he was American and were intent on having fun at his expense. " Hey, black man ! " they shouted. " 'Ello, very black, very black man ! "

Randy turned round. A year ago he'd have swung his fist; this time he waved. " *Le-bes!* " he greeted them in their own language, then turned to me with a tolerant grin. " They don't mean any harm, you know. The Moroccans are happy people. . . ."

Chapter Eight

Jester to the court of King Diz

You must know chord changes to sing jazz, there's no
in or out; you must pay the dues.

BABS GONZALES

Jester to the court of King Diz

The people who make jazz, be they mean, moody or magnanimous, are often as flamboyant and outlandish as the
music itself. The personal idiosyncrasies of some men match
the extent of their talent, witness Jelly Roll Morton, one of
the most influential figures in jazz, who not only claimed to
have invented the thing but strutted about, the picture of
sartorial elegance, with a flashing diamond set in gold in his
front incisor, another for a tiepin, and diamonds on his fingers,
as cuff-links and, so they say, "pinned to his underwear".

On the other hand, there are the jazz people whose influence can at best be described as minor, yet who are well
known to musicians and listeners alike, either by dint of
their ubiquity or, again, for their individualistic habits. You'd
have to be hard-pressed to ignore the wealth of legend that
surrounds the noted singer and humourist, Babs Gonzales,
who is said to have once caused a minor furore on the Champs
Elysées by appearing in an orange, brown and purple check
coat of excessive length, a black shirt and chrome-yellow bow-
tie, with a grey and red check beret topping the whole con-
fection like the cherry on a trifle.

The magniloquent Gonzales lives and works in compara-
tive obscurity nowadays but back in the times when bop was
gradually replacing the old order, the singer was a permanent
fixture of the scene. He first made an impact on the sensitivity
of the jazz public in the mid 'forties with a scat-happy vocal
group known as the Three Bips and a Bop which owed its
humorous approach if not its style to Leo Watson's Spirits of
Rhythm of the previous decade. Gonzales's partner-in-crime
during the initial stages of the combo's success was the pianist
Tadd Dameron, whose aptitude for humorous vocalising was
quickly forgotten when eclipsed by his important contributions
in the field of arranging.

As a singer, the raucous-voiced Gonzales is no Joe Williams

or Jimmy Witherspoon, but he has ears, he swings, and is one of the few people who can be unequivocally described as a *jazz* singer — period. He more or less originated an easy route to vocal improvisation which is still employed by jazz aspirants the world over — any time you hear scat singing in the " Oop-Pop-a-Da " vein you're hearing Gonzales — and although no important influence otherwise, he fulfilled a somewhat quaint function back in the bebop days as Jester to the Court of King Diz. Gillespie, incidentally, was successful with recordings of several Gonzales numbers.

He was born near New York, in New Jersey on 27 October 1919. " I'm from Newark, baby, across the river. My mother ran a boarding house and all the cats used to stay there out of Basie's band and Lunceford's, and I met 'em so I guess that was probably what started me to liking music.

" I started off playing the piano and then I switched to the tubs — the drums — and then it became too tiring. When I had my Three Bips and a Bop I was playing drums and singing all the things. It wasn't no set voice either, because certain tunes I might be the baritone or the contralto because of my pipes being like that. We just switched parts, Tadd and all of us. So when I started singing I looked at Billy Eckstine and all them cats and I said those cats can do it, so why not? And voilà — no sweat! And there's the beautiful part — no more lugging drums."

I recalled Lester Young's reason for giving up his own early career as a drummer : all the available women had left with the other musicians before he could finish packing his drumkit at the end of the date. Gonzales nodded his emphatic understanding of the universal plight of percussionists.

" That's right, because by the time I'd pack up and under my arms be sweating, it's forty minutes gone and all the saxophones and the horns would be in the hotels with all the little girls and the cat's blinking the lights on me — ' All right, all ready? OK, let's go. I gotta go home! ' Rigor mortis! "

Gonzales's first name job was with Charlie Barnet in 1944. He toured with the alto saxophonist's big band for several weeks, but never recorded, mainly because Lena Horne was then the featured attraction. Never a one to pass up an opportunity for blowing his own metaphorical trumpet, Babs could not resist commenting, " My job was more or less to help Lena out vocally. She's a great lady, but during that time I probably didn't hit the floor over seven times in maybe nine weeks because I was down in the hall rehearsing Lena."

From Barnet he joined Lionel Hampton for a five-month stint — " the circus, the Hampton circus! It was a *terrible* band! " (Babs, like so many of his contemporaries, often uses a derogatory term as the highest praise.) " I learned a lot with Gates; he's a great showman."

Mention of the vibraharpist's little-known nickname reminded me that Gonzales, like Ben Webster and the late Lester Young, has an irresistible penchant for bestowing nicknames on all and sundry wherever he goes. From barman to bandleader, journalist to janitor, it's impossible to spend half an hour with the singer and escape without a new and individual alias. " And why not? " he demanded. " They give 'em to *me* all the time."

He went on to explain how his own name came about. " My brothers are basketball players and they weigh 200 and 190 respectively. There was a basketball star in America called Big Babbiad, and so they were called Big Babs, Middle-sized Babs, and I'm Little Babs, and it just stayed. And then everybody looks when you say, ' Hey, Babs! ' and can you imagine one of my brothers — 200 pounds — walking down the street and he turns round and says, ' What? ' and all the women look because it's a girl's name. But that's crazy and I can't shake it.

" My real name is Lee Brown, and I picked Gonzales when I was with Charlie because they was Jim Crowing me in ofay hotels on the road and so I said if it's just simple enough to change my last name — why not? Get in the crazy hotels and sleep with the ofays. They think I'm Cubano and I can speak the language, too. So it stuck and only my real close people know my expubidence." (And that, in the correct Gonzales spelling, is his way of describing originality or soulful individualism.)

When Gonzales left the Hampton band in 1945, bop was busily getting into its stride. Uptown Minton's which had seen the gradual birth of the music was the hang-out for all the younger musicians and so the singer decided that his particular brand of musical humour could not fail to fill the bill. He took a group into the club for four weeks and ended up staying forty-one.

" I decided I'd ask the man for a raise and he said, ' Well, Babs, when I was playing I got three dollars a night and now the Union says I got to give you cats fifty for the leader and forty-two for the sidemen, and that's seven dollars a night. That's all you're gonna get. I've made more money off you than I ever made in existence but you ain't gonna get a quarter raise. Quit if you wanna — there's 200 cats waiting for this gig.' So I came out and went to Buffalo and stayed there about four months till rigor mortis set in. I went back to Minton's and stayed there till 1947 when I made the records for Alfred [Alfred Lion of Blue Note], the ' Oop-Pop-a-Da ' and things."

Gonzales's first records were made that February in the company of the altoist Rudy Williams, pianist Tadd Dameron, who also sang, the guitarist and vocalist Pee Wee Tinney, Art Phipps on bass and Charles Simon, drums. Titles were " Low-Pow ", " Oop-Pop-a-Da ", " Stomping at the Savoy ", " Pay Dem Blues ", and without Williams and the drummer, " Running Around ", " Babs's Dream ", " Dob Bla Bli " and " Weird Lullaby ". To most jazz enthusiasts the revelation of Dameron's presence on these early slices of zoot-suit era hip and humour has always come as a surprise but Gonzales, in his characteristically casual way, easily explained how he first met the composer of such classics as " Good Bait ", " Our Delight " and " Ladybird ".

" He was in New York rehearsing Sarah [Vaughan]. Well, Sarah's from my home; we went to school and grew up together — you dig? So I liked what Tadd was doing, I liked his harmonic structures and everything, and this was when Sarah made a record called ' If You Could See Me Now ' " [this, one of Miss Vaughan's first recordings, used Dameron's charts], " so Tadd was mainly writing.

" So one day he came to my rehearsal and Bobby Tucker didn't show up because he had went to work for Lady Day

[Billie Holiday]. So I said, ' Tadd, if you can sing and play you got yourself a gig, and that'll give you more variety for your writing.' So he said, ' I'm terrible, Babs, I'm very expubident ', and I said all right, and Tadd came on in the group. He was good, not as a lead singer, but for four or five part harmony, very cool."

The personnel of Gonzales's groups changed constantly. " Cats would get better gigs downtown and I'd have to get cats to replace them. At times I'd have nothing but guitar, bass and piano because this was the time when the happenings was happening and so many cats flew in and out."

Some of the later recordings featured a wide range of notables, among them J. J. Johnson, Art Pepper, Budd Johnson, Roy Haynes and Don Redman. Sonny Rollins first entered a recording studio under Gonzales's leadership, waxing " Capitolising " and " Professor Bop " in 1949, and the following year saw a session which featured, oddly enough, the vocal talents of pianist Wynton Kelly. Said Babs : " Wynton can sing like crazy and he can play the fiddle, too. Sometimes what you least expect will be what'll gas you, but I always knew who could play and who couldn't. A lot of cats don't get a chance to make records. So when I get a chance and I know cats can cook, I go get 'em."

In spite of the fact that Gonzales updates his material by throwing contemporary references into his scat and by writing songs a little more representative of the current day, his style, like his mode of dress and his outrageous line in jive-talk, is basically as dated as the zoot-suit or the jitterbug. But back in the 'forties it was a different story. Bebop was the thing that year and the year after and the one after that. The music was new and vital and the Gonzales forefinger was firmly on the hipster's pulse. As the exuberant singer felt it — " I was excited very *crazi-l-ly*!

" It excited me so much that you can see where I am — voilà! But you see they couldn't get no money [out of the music] till the ' Oop-Pop-a-Da ' popped, and that's where I came in to give it to the public." Gonzales's Blue Note recording of the song sold a mere 45,000 because of the label's then limited facilities for distribution, but Lady Luck smiled more kindly on the later version made by the Gillespie big band.

"One day Dizzy was auditioning for Victor at the Down-beat and I was right next door at the Onyx," said Babs, recalling two of the major clubs on the old Fifty-second Street. "But the cats there didn't dig him and he came in and he was so drug that I said, 'Man, bring your trumpets and John Lewis in here and just put my group in there with your expubidence and the ofays aren't going to know any different. We'll do "Oop-Pop-a-Da".' So I just sang my tune with Dizzy and my group for the audition before I left town. About two weeks later when I was in Chicago — boom! Atom Bomb! Dizzy sold about 700,000 copies for Victor. The bread was cool from my point of view, but I'm glad that Birksy could get his big band behind it instead of scuffling."

He continued, nonchalantly: "After that I went out with Dizzy's big band and even took my whole group. The money was low but we had to keep it rolling. I kind of stayed like as a compact of Dizzy's thing without no billing just to keep it moving after 'Oop-Pop' popped for him. I stayed about three months and then I said, 'Well, crazy, man, I got to go on back and take care of mine', and so I put Joe Carroll in my place.

"When I came back to New York looking for gigs, rigor mortis set in for about eight or nine months. Then I joined a group called the Manhattan Singers to come to Europe." There, Babs ran into saxophonist James Moody in Sweden and so began, in 1951, a partnership that was to last for three years.

"'Moody's Mood' put Moody over the fence when we was up here in Sweden and stuff, and then I made two good ones with him called the 'Cool Whalin'' [*sic*] and 'The James Moody Story'. So all through that time when we played before a crowd of people they expect to hear you come out and sing those three tunes or some one of them. This is some-thing I learnt from Hamp — no matter how much a cat can blow, the crowd will go berserk and want their money back if they can't hear that special tune. You got to sing them, it's part of the dues."

Gonzales is proud that the majority of the songs in his

repertoire are his own compositions, with the exception of
" The Preacher ", " A Night In Tunisia " and " Round Midnight ", the lyrics to these being written, he says, " on request
from Horace [Silver], Birksy and Thelonious " [the composers].
" But," he insists, " I do nothing of anybody else's. I don't like
any people that copies."

Although he is always associated with the idiom known as
" vocalese " where words are fitted to a previously recorded
instrumental line, Babs kicks hard against this inference. As
far as he is concerned, " The things I write have not been
solos, they have been musical words. I want to clear that up
quick 'cause the things like Lambert, Hendricks and (I'll say
Ross 'cause that was *it*) were doing have hit me in the face.
They're very clever but I just don't like people that copies.
I know Paul — whatshisname — Quinichette copied Lester
Young note for note, but even if you're a painter and you
ain't got no expubidence, you don't get no hellos from Gonzales! "

Of the few singers who made a speciality of vocalese —
they include Annie Ross and Eddie Jefferson — the best
known is Clarence Beeks, who is even better known as King
Pleasure. His vocal version of a James Moody improvisation
on " I'm In The Mood For Love " is a classic of its kind but
Gonzales, who now claims Pleasure as a friend, admits that at
one time because of his appropriation of what was virtually a
routine devised by Moody and himself, " we were the *deadliest*
of enemies.

" He used to follow me and Moody around from town to
town and so we said we'd get this cat a gig 'cause he's serious,
you dig? Everywhere you look there he is! So anyway, when
his record of ' Moody's Mood ' came out, we were in California. So he didn't want to give Moody his bread. He had
claimed the whole tune after having been with us! But when
we got back to New York, all it takes is a little New York
consultation . . ." (here the singer produced a small plastic
bottle filled with his famous red pepper, just one of the many
weapons with which he protects himself against real or
imagined assault, and laughed ominously). " And so now we're
the most *beautiful* of friends."

Gonzales could hardly be described as a man of half-hearted opinions. His ideas about what constitutes a jazz singer are firmly entrenched. He considers that the majority of vocalists tagged with the jazz label are, in reality, better described as folk-singers, and he holds out vehemently against the lady singers of the so-called " cool " school.

" The only jazz singers I heard in my life were the First Lady — Ella Fitzgerald — Carmen McRae, Annie Ross and myself," he declared. " People like Joe Carroll and Eddie Jefferson are riff singers, scat singers, and there's a difference. They followed Leo Watson.

" Take all them broads — they put a stamp on Chris Connor and that other broad, June Christy — they all followed Anita O'Day. But look like they could have heard that Anita was singing out of tune. I ain't never heard Chris Connor sing in tune yet! I figure if they dropped her off the Cliffs of Dover she wouldn't sing in tune, after all these years. Really, I'm serious.

" You must know chord changes to sing jazz, there's no in or out; you must pay the dues. So if you don't know the chord changes there's no way you can run 'em. Now Sarah knows the chords from the piano but she can't swing. She sings good jazz ballads, but she can't come upstairs with Ella and Carmen and Annie — you dig? I mean with the *fire*."

And the same incorrect categorising has ruined Oscar Brown Jr's image, according to Gonzales. " He don't belong. He's a folk-singer and a very clever lyricist, but they did him a great disservice when they touted him as a jazz singer. Everywhere he hit the stage people were looking for him to sing jazz and he'd come out in a sweat-shirt talking about the Mississippi River! "

To spend a half-hour in conversation with " Terrible " Gonzales is to live temporarily in another world, the world of the night people, the gamblers, the showmen, the sportsmen, the whores and the pimps, the world that is alternately flamboyant and seedy. The word " flamboyant ", in fact, could have been invented with him in mind, for the irresistible singer is an extravagant individualist from the top of his crazily groomed head to the pointed tips of his Italian boots.

When he walks in a room, any room, it's more than likely that Babs will know at least half the people there, and if he doesn't, within five minutes flat he will. Fast-talking, quick-thinking, scandal-mongering and inquisitive to the point of downright nosiness, Babs Gonzales is the hustler supreme. He goes everywhere, does everything, knows everybody who is anybody and plenty that are nowhere. If you want to know what's cooking uptown or downtown in New York or in Paris or London and Gonzales is around, he'll hip you in less time than it takes to ask.

And you'd never know if he was working or not, so audacious is his line in bigtime. In the past the manufacturer and retailer of an unorthodox item of menswear known as the Atomic Bowtie, his current line in merchandise is a gold-cardboard packaged record on his own Expubidence label, entitled " Tales On The Famous — Guess Who? " wherein the master of unsubtle satire details a series of incidents which befell a number of his well-known colleagues, past and present. The unfortunate victims of his verbal massacre barely survive under thinly-veiled pseudonyms.

In spite of his all too obvious lack of modesty, Gonzales would be the first to admit that his songs fall some way outside the Cole Porter class, yet he continues to be a prolific and relatively successful writer. Wynton Kelly once laughingly recalled a session where one of Gonzales's tunes was committed to wax : " He always comes around hustling with his tunes — seems like he heard about the recording session even before we did ! "

" Gotta take care of business, baby " is the Gonzales slogan, and whether that entails entertaining, song-writing or peddling his recently published autobiography, *I Paid My Dues*, you can bet your life he'll be making the customers laugh with his irreverent comments on both the ugly and the beautiful sides of jazz and show business.

They don't make people like that any more.

Chapter Nine

The sweet smell of success

A note doesn't care who plays it — whether you're black,
white, green, brown or opaque!

CLARK TERRY

The sweet smell of success

When Duke Ellington played London in 1958, the fans backstage outnumbered the musicians. I was new to the one-upmanship game of " capturing the stars ", yet when a sharply-dressed trumpeter grinned my way from under a rakishly-tilted French beret, I swooped in the unmistakable manner of the European jazz fan at large. " Say, do you know where I could get a coffee? " he asked pleasantly as the other luckless musicians milled around, trying to look unperturbed in alien surroundings. Five minutes later we were sipping slopped-in-the-saucer *cappucino* and talking about the Ellington band. I thought I'd captured Clark Terry for a while and I couldn't believe my luck, but in reality that cunning gentleman, endowed with the requisite handful of Ellingtonian mystique, had ended up by devastatingly captivating me!

The remarkably unruffled Clark Terry consistently wins all the honours for being one of the most courteous and cheerful jazzmen of our time. Whether the voters be friends, fellow musicians or the fans who have only met his bubbling trumpet and effervescent fluegelhorn across the footlights, Clark has a knack of persuading them that his time is their own. He was the first musician to give me a glimpse of the world where the jazzmen live.

When it comes to his playing, few musicians dispense more handfuls of happiness than the dimpled ex-Ellingtonian, and whenever he stretches out, the promise of merriment that lurks in his twinkling eyes and in the crinkly grin that plays perpetually around the corners of his lips is faithfully relayed through his volatile horns.

For the past ten years Clark has been a staff musician at NBC Television in New York City. This enviable position guarantees him a regular and relatively substantial income on the one hand, and represents on the other the overturning of yet another barrier built by prejudice. He has a nation-wide reputation as a dependable and talented session man, not to mention an instantly recognisable solo style, but in such a racially tense society as America you don't stop paying your dues the moment success lifts you up in the palm of its hand. The trumpeter knows this, and realises that when dealing with what he calls " the nine-to-five people " you have to stay in a " business mood " and be forever on your toes.

There is still some opposition to his presence in the studios where Clark's is a familiar and sometimes unwelcome face. " That's something that's been going on for a very long time in this business. It's pretty ridiculous but it still exists," he admitted. " There are people who refer to us as ' them ', saying, ' They don't fit ' or ' They can't play our type of music ', and so on, but of course there was also a time when Negroes used to brand any Caucasian jazz players as sad. But the way I see it, a note doesn't care who plays it. If you play it good, you play it good, if you play it bad, you play it bad — whether you're black, white, green, brown or opaque!

" Some people in the studios do look out for your mistakes and so on, but they wouldn't come out in the open about it. That's the work of a coward and you know a coward never works out in the open. He's sort of a night creature, but as the jargon goes, there's always somebody who's out to get you."

Clark's financial stability enables him to continue playing jazz, his first love, as and when he wishes. Outside the studios, he works regularly with his trombonist sidekick, Bob Brook-meyer, and accepts the occasional weekend date for his own big band, a unit which is made up mainly of fellow session men. Enjoyment is the prime motivation in these engagements, economic considerations a minor point. His services as soloist, session man, leader and contractor for record dates are constantly in demand, and as a consequence the trumpeter commutes with ease from studio to nightclub. This state of affairs he calls " a completely different bag " from the life of the average musician, but that he still regards himself primarily as a jazzman was obvious when he went on to explain that : " We jazz players live on the other side of the clock. Doing the work I do, though, I have to live on both sides of the clock. You snatch and grab rest whenever, wherever and however, so it's an interesting way of earning a living, but a hard one, too."

But finding the time to snatch forty winks is far from being the trumpeter's only problem; he has heavy dues to pay in yet another area. Having almost single-handedly broken down the discrimination that existed in television, he now faces the jibes of certain "soul brothers" who accuse him of pandering to Whitey and trading his soul and musical ideals in exchange for his steady berth.

Debonair and relaxed, Clark has for this, as always, a considered reply. "I hate to think this, but there have been rumours that cats have put me down and said all sorts of weird things like 'He's down there with *them*' — whatever they mean by 'them'. I don't know whether it's because I rarely get a chance to work in Harlem where my fellow brothers are for the most part located, but there are a few envious people in that part of town. I just don't have occasion to go there."

One thing is certain, Clark Terry's no fool. When his increased employment as a sideman on record dates made him an obvious candidate for staff session work, he realised that the fingers would continue to wag from both sides of the fence when he made the move, and so he adjusted accordingly. Abrasive comments do little to dent the good-humoured veneer concealing a much more complex person, for Clark has sophistication on his side and that can overcome a multitude of problems. For many musicians the idea of working outside the familiar oblivion of the smoke-filled nightclub would be absolute anathema, but not for this one. He revels in the good things of life : the hand-tailored shirts, the custom-made shoes, the taste of old cognac, the sweet smell of success. Clark Terry lives with the kind of luxury that money *can* buy, yet by virtue of the unimpaired quality of his jazz, he is also able to cock a snook at the sceptics who denigrate his chosen way of life.

"There are a lot of cats who sort of put you down if you play studio type music," he explained. "They refer to you as a square and as one who has gone over to the other side. They got all sort of things to call you, but for the most part the guys

who complain to this extent are guys who either haven't prepared themselves to do a wide variety of work, or guys who
just don't really care to do it because they think it's unhip. But
as for my jazz ability, it reminds me of that old saying, 'Do
you read music?' and the guy would say, 'Not enough to
hurt my playing!' I hope it hasn't affected mine and I still
try to keep abreast of everything that is happening."

In spite of his spry and youthful appearance, the trumpeter
is fast approaching middle age, a time when, for many, bore-
dom has begun to set in and curb creativity. Clark, who could
easily qualify for the title of " the youngest grandfather in
jazz ", finds that he enjoys music more now than at any time
in the past. " There was a time when it was so necessary to
stay in more or less one trend of thought in order to do what
was the most important thing, that is, to make a living out of
music, but after a few years on a more lucrative scene, you
find that you're freer," he explained. " In other words, you're
a little more free to think and concentrate on jazz when you
don't have to concentrate on filling yours and the rest of your
family's stomachs. It's been said many times that a lot of the
best jazz comes out of hungry players, but I don't know about
that. For musicians, it's pretty hard to blow on an empty
stomach."

It was during the 'fifties that the recording studios first
opened their doors to the persistent knocking of the jazz
musicians. Until then they were a discounted breed for anything other than jazz, for the powers-that-be refused to believe
that any purely instinctive player could also tackle a compli-
cated score. Prior to overcoming such narrow thinking, the
St Louis-born trumpeter had served with the cream of the
big bands — Count Basie, Duke Ellington, Lionel Hampton,
Quincy Jones, Charlie Barnet and Eddie Vinson — and done
more than his fair share of reading with them. " I never made
any effort to get into the studios," he said, " it just came
about. I was in at the beginning of a new time and I found
it quite interesting. It was quite a challenge, and for a con-
scientious person who likes to get with his axe, it's another
avenue to travel."

The jazz world has a pretty high opinion of Clark Terry

and he, in turn, holds his compatriots in the highest esteem. " In this business it's been proven that you can take a guy out of the symphony and sit him in a jazz group, but even if he has some jazz background, he can't really make it. But if a guy has studied his instrument well enough and is jazz orientated, you can take him out of a jazz band and stick him in with the classics, and if he can read well enough and has a good tone, he can blend and fit and play right along with the topnotch classical players. Benny Goodman went to great lengths to prove this, and so I think that people in the studios know very well that the jazz players, for the most part, are also qualified to play various types of music. And nine times out of ten I think they're better musicians for the job."

The trumpeter also bowed to Goodman for establishing another precedent which led eventually to the respect for the sensitivity of the jazzman's reading. " He never particularly cared for a lead trumpet unless he could play jazz, because this was the type of player who could interpret more swingingly than the strictly legitimate type player who would have a tendency to be rigid, tense and not too loose. In order to play that brand of swinging jazz lead you have to be pretty free. As a matter of fact, in the first band I was associated with, the George Hudson band, I played lead. I was sort of a chief cook and bottle-washer — lead player, soloist, comedian, everything ! "

Generally speaking, a musician of Clark's calibre can pick and choose his dates so that he is not saddled with mediocre music to play. " Most of the time, though, you're not going to be playing jazz," he affirmed. " And you may find yourself playing all sorts of garbage ! If you face it like it's another task, and try not to hurry and forget about what it is, do it in the manner the leader is asking you to do it, the next time he calls you — which I'm sure he will if you did a good job — he may give you an interesting piece to play. But if you don't play it well, next time he *won't* call you."

Getting back to another of his virtues, Clark Terry considers that musicians today are far more generous with their time and knowledge than they were when he was coming up. " I had a pretty rough time as a young boy in my home town.

The older musicians were rather cruel, they wouldn't give you the right answers, and of course I found it rather difficult to come by a decent instrument, being from a large, poor family." As a result of this, the trumpeter vowed that if he ever had the chance to help the less fortunate, he would do so whenever and wherever he could and, true to his word, he has helped several aspiring young trumpeters, even to the point of buying them instruments.

"With the older cats there was always the fear that a younger musician would reach a plateau where he could compete with you," recalled Clark. "They would say, 'The same words that you used to a youngster are going to come back at you.' These were the old fogey-ism type cats, you know." He agreed that their reasons probably had an economic basis. "As a matter of fact, I'm sure that was why, because if there were twenty guys playing one instrument there usually weren't twenty jobs available.

"Years ago the reason many Negroes didn't read music was because the older people were always told, 'There's no point in you learning to read because you'll never get a job in a symphony orchestra or anything of that sort, anyhow.' So they used to tell you to learn to play jazz, to play what you feel. You can't say that they didn't study because learning to improvise, you know, that's quite a study in itself, but they didn't actually devote much time to reading music off paper because there actually was no future for them."

Today, Clark's attitude towards the extent of integration in the more respected areas of music is a magnanimous one, in spite of the fact that in 1968 out of 180 musicians in New York's three television orchestras, only nine were black. There are still many changes to be made, but at least he can be proud of being a pioneer. It's hardly surprising that he almost breathes a sigh of relief when recalling how he refused to be daunted by the die-hard attitude of St Louis' "old fogeys".

"I was one of those stupid ones," he said with a sarcastic smile. "I didn't believe people when they told me that you didn't need to learn to read. I felt that I might just want to see what this other guy's doing, so I went ahead and tried. Of course, I couldn't have lessons because, as I said before, I could hardly come by an instrument that was decent enough to play on, but I practised more or less on my own and by the time I got half-grown, there were all sorts of things available for reading."

This same tenacity of purpose has been evident throughout the trumpeter's career. That he has succeeded in finding both fame and fortune is unusual enough in itself, but so also is the merry way he has moved towards his goal. Anyone who is halfway familiar with the jazzman's daily dues knows full well that the grinning, extrovert musician is a stereotype as out of date as last year's kisses. The pressures that society brings to bear on the creative artist in America are so great it's a wonder that anybody wants to play happy music today; but they do. Clark Terry is one of the happy ones and with reason. In 1969 he confounded his critics by organising regular music sessions for deprived Harlem youngsters. Once again Clark Terry did the right thing at the right time, but the laugh was on his critics. By giving something of himself, once again, he was also giving hope to young musicians.

Chapter Ten

A question of influence

It doesn't mean a thing to me to be classed as a member of the avant garde. I think that it's just a term they're sticking on to a form of music like they stuck bebop on to Charlie Parker's music.

JACKIE MCLEAN

A question of influence

The most salutary fact about jazz is that it is essentially a music which gives an opportunity for every voice to be heard. Musicians themselves recognise this, and because of it they rarely " put down " or denigrate a fellow improviser. " I make it a rule never to say anything that reflects on a person's means of making a living," Ornette Coleman has said, yet some of the listeners will quote their table of who-influenced-whom in the jazz lineage at the drop of a hat.

This tedious catechism has disrupted the recognition of many potentially fine musicians, especially those who grew up in the postwar period and were inescapably affected by the all-pervading cry of Charlie Parker's alto saxophone. That his spell was not cast on saxophonists alone is suggested by a statement once made by the Ellington trumpeter, Cootie Williams, a perceptive if rarely vocal critic: " He did more for jazz than any one musician I can think of and he also hurt it more, because there were so many musicians who loved him and idolised him until all the instruments copied after him. The drums, the bass, the piano — every instrument in the band wanted to play like Charlie Parker."

Jackie McLean, who was just sixteen when he met Parker in 1947, has had more than his fair share of personal problems. Prejudice, poverty and narcotics have all ganged up to take sufficient emotional toll of the still young saxophonist without him also having to shoot down the people who shut their ears to his imperious originality, yet Jackie, a substantial and highly exciting player in his own right, was hampered for years by the " Bird-imitator " tag. Only now is the alto saxophonist acclaimed as one of the major jazz soloists, a man who is out front in the avant garde without relinquishing his position in the mainstream. True, he admits, he wanted to sound like Bird as a teenager, but that, after all, is only the usual process of influence preceding the finding of oneself.

" In fact, I thought it was unreligious to play unless you played like Bird !

" But," he affirmed, " I think that the people who called me an imitator never really did any real listening of their own. As hard as I tried, I don't think I ever really sounded like Bird. It was in 1947–48 that I sounded as close as I could and even when I recorded with Miles in 1949, I'd already started to change." He is caustically outspoken about the critical qualifications of the people who dismissed him as a copyist : " A lot of critics that come on the scene now don't seem to listen. They seem to wait and jump on a bandwagon the minute they hear somebody who seems to know what they're talking about. To make a statement that is very raw and plain, I think that many writers are full of shit. I'd like to interview some of the writers as a musician just to find out where they're at ! But coming back to Bird, that's old hat in a way. I haven't heard anybody refer to him as far as I'm concerned, recently."

Jackie McLean is a highly sensitive and intelligent man, slow to smile unless there's something to smile about, yet relaxed and amenable, warm in his own way. You get the impression that he's always been an adult, and growing up in Harlem, the cruellest survival-of-the-fittest jungle of them all, it was easy for childhood to pass him by. The seriousness and the sensitivity have always been there, according to those who have known him since his early days; so has the music. His father, John McLean, was a guitarist with the Tiny Bradshaw band, but Jackie hardly remembers him; his initial musical tuition came from his godfather. " From around the age of six I used to go to church with him every Sunday and sit next to him while he played for the services. That's how I more or less got introduced to the saxophone," he recalled.

At the age of fourteen-and-a-half his godfather gave him one of his two soprano saxophones, and for his fifteenth birthday, an alto. " My stepfather at that time listened to a lot of jazz. He listened to Louis Armstrong, Count Basie and Duke Ellington, and when I heard that, I liked Lester Young and Ben Webster." Jackie says that he didn't care for the conventional alto saxophone sound. " My stepfather would say, ' This is how you play ', and he'd put on a record by Duke's big band

and I'd hear Johnny Hodges or Willie Smith, but there was something about the timbre of the instrument that I just didn't like. So, I began to play the alto in a deep register and try to emulate Lester Young, that type of thing, until a year or so later when my father bought a record shop and we were bringing in some new stock. I put on this record by Trummy Young, Dizzy Gillespie and Charlie Parker, and that was the first time I heard Bird. The name of the record was ' Seventh Avenue' and ' Sorta Kinda' and that sort of changed my whole concept. In actual fact, though, I heard Dexter Gordon before I heard Charlie Parker. I used to play like his solo on ' Blowin' the Blues Away', Billy Eckstine's big band thing."

Although Jackie elected to spend his life with the alto more than twenty years ago, he has continually railed against what is for him the over-lush swing era sound as typified by Willie Smith and Johnny Hodges. He modelled his own sound entirely on the tenor saxophonists Lester Young and Dexter Gordon until he realised that Parker had dispensed with the conventional wide vibrato and brought about a one-man tonal revolution. Jackie, who was later to become a close personal friend of Bird's, met him through pianist Bud Powell, with whom he was studying on weekends. Soon he began to follow Parker wherever he was playing.

" I got to know him through being a fan of his, you know, and we'd talk, but the first time he really recognised meeting me was after a year when I'd been pestering him to get me in here and get me in there because I was under age. I talked to him quite a bit right up to the time he died, first about kid things, then as I grew up we began to discuss the problems of manhood. By the time I was eighteen he knew me pretty well and I guess he was wondering because Bud had told him I was coming along pretty fast on the horn."

Jackie had grown up fast in every way. Harlem had helped him along and hanging out with the older musicians enlarged his horizons. Narcotics addiction at the age of seventeen completed the trick. Two years later he was playing regularly with Miles Davis and holding his own. " Miles influenced me with his choice of notes and the way he played, even though I couldn't copy anything directly from his concept," he recalled, and his precociousness made him a figure of interest for Parker. It was not long before his idol was actually asking him to substitute for him when two dates coincided, a compliment that fazed even Jackie, at that time the original blasé " hippie ". " I'd go and hold down the job till he got there. Things like that I'm pretty proud of, you know," he confided. " I stayed pretty close to him until he died."

Around 1952, three years before the death of his mentor, Jackie discovered that his own concept was changing. " I began to feel differently about what I was playing." Bird's influence was still heady but Jackie noticed a change coming " from within the horn itself ", especially when he ran himself into an improvisational blind alley. " Things that Bird would play, I'd try to find something different to play. It probably wasn't too far away from his style but it was more or less getting into something that was mine." At that time, the tenor saxophonist Sonny Rollins, his close friend and colleague from all the little gigs of teenage days, was himself having a strong influence on Jackie's playing. " Although," he admitted, " Charlie Parker had a strong influence on him, too, so it's the same kind of thing."

The jazz life is generously tinged with irony and so it was hardly surprising that when Jackie was finding his feet in spite of the personal problems that held him in bondage, the critics' barbs hit home the hardest. As his superior playing won him a larger audience for his virile alto, so the accusations of plagiarism mounted. " I tried to express myself and the things that I used to hear myself, but I can honestly say that Bird never influenced me to do anything wrong. He never taught me anything directly about music, but more or less I was just so much around him and his playing. We never talked about music too much, the only music I got was from listening to him play."

Jackie has always been an emotional player, his searing, incisive alto fairly stinging with the heartfelt cry of the underprivileged. There's a lot of anger in there, too, something that he, like Cecil Taylor, accounts for by saying : " These are rebellious times in this country. When I play I rebel against everything I dislike in this society, the whole system. And sometimes people come up to me and they're very drug because I sounded so angry. It happens, but there are plenty of moments when I feel other things, too."

The Jackie McLean of today is a man of contrasts. Pale, full-bearded, young yet mature, running to fat and self-confessedly lazy yet somehow poised and with an attitude of superiority. His personal life has changed radically since he wrenched himself from dependence on drugs, yet the fire and the anger of his music have never abated. " A lot of my past performances have been very emotional because I wasn't putting any work into it and I hit the stage with no practice under my belt. It'd be an emotional performance because I'd be fighting with myself, trying to make things that wouldn't come out and really not doing it the right way."

The inevitable changes that the years have wrought in Jackie's diamond-hard music have lifted him right upfront where he is respected and regarded as one of the most hard-hitting, compelling saxophonists playing today. He reached this unassailable position for two reasons. One, a sense of responsibility to the music and a surprising personal integrity in the face of all obstacles (" Even when I was sick I always made time on the gig "), and two, the imperative way he strode to contemporaneity. Casting off the Parker mantle and donning the cloak of McLean was never a conscious move. " I could never sit down and think of changing just like that," he insisted. " There are still times today that I listen to Charlie Parker and things come back to me in my mind and I'll find myself, on my next job or something, referring to some of his phrases before I'll admit it."

His major preoccupation in the autumn of 1967 was to produce a satisfactory sound from his saxophone. " I've found that my sound, as far as its bigness is concerned, is hampering my speed. So I've changed my mouthpiece around a little bit and I've made my sound just a little more crystal so that I could get more out of the instrument without sounding bogged down or syrupy. That's the thing I've always tried to do, that's what kept my sound original. The alto saxophone has a funny tendency to be awfully sweet and syrupy if you don't approach it with a certain thing in mind, and even though my horn *isn't* sweet and syrupy, it tends to get that way to me if I sound like I sounded three years ago. So I've been working on getting a more lighter thing."

His early début on the jazz scene is indicative of an adventurous spirit, and in that respect Jackie is still an explorer. As early as 1955 he was writing tunes without conventional chord progressions, even if he was unable to improvise freely on them at the time. "I was pretty hung up with chord changes then," he admitted. As a result, he would invent a set of chord changes to improvise on for the spontaneous passages, in spite of the fact that the tune was chordless. It was the advent of Ornette Coleman some four years later that inspired him to dispense with these leaning-posts. "His concept, theoretically, appealed to me a great deal as far as just being able to play the instrument from a purely emotional standpoint. So today, right up to now, I'm sort of, like, just practising very hard to get the instrument even more under my fingers. I find that I can't get the different sounds I want to produce by the technique that I used to use, say, three years ago. So now it's just like an open cross-country race, where everybody's trying to get as much out of the instrument as they can."

He explained his essentially spontaneous approach to improvisation : " First you have to have complete command of the instrument and then you leave the rest to your emotions. You go where your emotions take you. When I play I listen closely to the rhythm section and play exactly how I feel and then, too, if you have a melody in the beginning or some sort of form, a statement that you can go back to in the end, you can play from that."

In some ultra-radical circles, Jackie is thought of as a " stone bebopper at heart ", a fact that does nothing to damage his reputation as an iconoclast. Jackie *is* avant garde, he doesn't need to belong to a movement to prove it. What the pedants probably mean, as they slosh about in their semantic swamp, is that Jackie prefers to play a variety of material and does not feel compelled to stay " outside " for an entire evening. " I play some things that you can't snap your fingers to because the time is free, completely open," he said. " You're not sup-

posed to snap your fingers at it. Then I play some tunes that
are very much *that* way," he snapped his fingers on two and
four descriptively. " Then nights will go by when I won't play
a blues. Like one time my bass player, Scotty Holt, came to
me on intermission and said, ' Jackie, do you realise we've
been here four days and we haven't played a blues? ' I hadn't
thought of it and I said, ' Wow ! ' The next set I went up on
the stand and played a real Lester Young–Charlie Parker-type
blues and I enjoyed it and so did the audience."

Anyone who has heard half a chorus of the vital Jackie
McLean will know that his exuberant alto bristles constantly
with the blues even if he slips away from the blues format. It
is hardly surprising that this is his credo : " The blues feeling
is part of jazz, and I even hear the blues in the greatest of
European composers, people like Bartok that I love so much.
You can hear the blues in their lines, but I think that if you
go so far away from the blues, you'll be reaching a point
where European music and jazz as we know it will eventually
meet. If you take avant garde jazz and the very contemporary
classical composers you'll see that that's it. I probably won't
even be alive when that happens, but as long as I play jazz
I'll always have that blues feeling. That's for *sure*."

That's one influence no jazzman in his right mind wants
to escape.

Chapter Eleven

One for Buck

If you don't do something new, then you might as well
forget it.

BUCK CLAYTON

One for Buck

There used to be a theory that jazz musicians reached their creative peak around the forty mark and then spent the rest of their lives coasting or basking in the shadow of their former glory. In the unpredictable world of jazz, though, men don't live according to the book — and that's the beauty of it. Nothing, in fact, gives me greater pleasure than standing back and watching the theorists squirm when someone like Buck Clayton is doing the upsetting. He does it so adroitly.

"The prettiest man I ever saw", according to the late Billie Holiday, Buck is one of the truly timeless jazzmen. There is nothing dated about his bountiful middle-of-the-road trumpet style, in spite of the fact that he has been playing professionally since 1932 and saw service with the epoch-making Count Basie band of 1936–43. On the contrary, the freshness of his essentially optimistic horn stems directly from a young man's mind. The debonair son of Parsons, Kansas, has refused to allow time to pass him by.

Wilbur "Buck" Clayton, otherwise known as "Cat Eye" in deference to his brilliant green eyes, was born in 1911 when jazz was already a decade old. "Music," he explained in his gentle Western accent, "is something I've wanted to do since I was a little kid. It's something I've grown up with, grown alongside. I was one of the few people fortunate to grow up to be exactly what I wanted to be."

During his seven years with Basie, Buck was one of the outstanding soloists in the most famous band that included Lester Young, Harry Edison, Herschel Evans and Dicky Wells. In 1943 his career was abruptly terminated by his conscription, but from an immediate postwar stint with Jazz at the Philharmonic on its first nation-wide tour, he has gone so literally from strength to strength that he's only just reaching the summit of his artistry. Buck, as one of the most enduring jazz people, is a harbinger of joy and a constantly creative

musician. As for his instantly recognisable tone, it is alternately as brittle as glass and as plush as purple velvet.

The trumpeter credits his two children, Stephen and
Candis, with being the reason for his youthfulness, and is
almost reticently modest with regard to his continuing zest
for music. " I've heard many times that when you get to a
certain age you're supposed to stop," he smiled, almost apolo-
getically, " but the only thing I can think is that people get
used to one instrument. I know people who have a horn made
twenty years ago and they've been using it for fifteen and
don't want to change. In the meantime, the instrument companies keep progressing and making better horns."

Buck himself is a strong believer in change. " There are
many trumpet players who've been playing the same mouthpiece since 1935 and they won't dare change! But I'll get a
new one tomorrow if I think it will be better — at least I'll
give it a try. Other than that, I don't know if my actual
musical ideas alter, but the ability to execute some of them
improves with a newer mouthpiece or a new trumpet."

Buck is a good deal more fortunate than many of his
associates who rose to fame on the crest of the swing wave
and have, with the years, found their music utterly outmoded.
Some musicians work infrequently and seldom in sympathetic
surroundings, but Buck, who is adept at taking care of business, has a beautiful home out on New York's Long Island
where he lives when he's not working and, what's more, lives
well. He works ten months out of the year, mostly as a featured
soloist, and organises his own groups for frequent trips to
Europe and Canada. The trumpeter generally calls the tune.

" I think I can adapt to pretty well anybody," he maintained when discussing some of the obstacles he encounters
when working as a " single ". " I've played with a lot of
guys who can play nothing but Dixieland and again with a
lot of guys who play nothing but modern jazz, although," he
added with a smile, " I've never played with any ' free form '
musicians. I don't think I'll ever make that."

Adaptability, both from a musical and personal standpoint,
has made working as a single Buck's most feasible proposition,
yet whenever the chance presents itself, he enjoys leading his

own band. However, as he pointed out : " If you don't work for a couple of weeks you've got to go and collect up your group again and you may find them on another job. Working as a soloist is an easier way to live."

In the jazz game there have never been enough jobs to go round for all the musicians, but the situation is especially tough on men of Buck's age today. He realises how fortunate he is that his phone rings so frequently that he can pick and choose his jobs, but since 1949 he has spent a sizeable chunk of his time in Europe. Money in America is better for a single week or a fortnight, but Buck calculates that he earns more in the long run by working across the Atlantic where he is well known and loved.

He was, in fact, one of the first jazz musicians to be more or less adopted by the French coterie of critics and admirers, and his first European tour took him all over France. " I was quite unknown then," he recalled. " When the house wasn't but one-third full they'd point at me and say, ' *inconnu* '. I started travelling earlier than most musicians who have been to Europe, I guess, so it's not like that now. If there's a festival going on or a big package tour, they'll call me first of all and I'm lucky in that. Now you take an artist today that may be very good. He could go over there, but regardless of his talent he would still be ' *inconnu* '. So starting out in 1949 has given me what you might call a little edge on the scene."

Buck's enthusiasm for the music has never abated, and neither has his urge to travel. The constant change of surroundings and company that broadens the mind is more responsible than anything else for keeping his music progressive. " I could have been on a studio job by now, but I wouldn't like sitting in one place, going to work and doing the same thing. If you do the same thing for fifteen, twenty years, getting up at the same time every morning, catching the same old train and coming home at the same time, it ages you."

The trumpeter saw an example of the ageing process during the war years. " When I went in the army I met guys who were younger than me but they thought and acted older. They were really young kids but because they had done nothing but work hard all their lives on the farm, they seemed to me about twenty years older than I was. It's the same with music. If someone's in town that I want to hear, I'll go out of my way to go to see them."

Buck's smile had a grateful edge to it. " I doubt if I'll ever get set in my ways. You know my kids — sometimes I have to bend over backwards to go along with what is coming up nowadays that wasn't there when I was their age. Things change. Everything alters from day to day and I just don't believe in sitting down and living in the past. Now I admire the past, I admire many things about it. Take the first time I ever heard Duke Ellington play ' The Mooche '; I admire that, but he doesn't play that way now, and I hope I don't either."

Jazz, wrote Whitney Balliett, is the sound of surprise, and the great men of the music have been, for the most part, instinctive improvisers. Even today, someone like Ornette Coleman relies on spontaneous combustion rather than carefully thought out patterns, and he is one of the most exciting artists the music has known. Buck, a far gentler player, is no exception to this unwritten rule. " I never think much about what I'm going to play, but unless I don't feel particularly good, everything comes out like I want it to come out. It's one of those things I can't explain.

" First of all, music is a ball. It's — what do you call it — self-inspiration. If nobody else is going to inspire you, you inspire yourself and you end up just playing. Usually, just blowing my horn, the first note to me is a satisfaction, and it's only at the times that you don't feel good that the horn becomes a problem. When you don't feel good that trumpet weighs about 150 pounds ! "

Buck first started listening to jazz at the tender age of six. " It started early and I hope it ends late ! " Even if he personally chose to remain in the " mainstream " period stylistically, he never closed his receptive mind to the subsequent course of jazz, and therein lies his major virtue. In addition, he stipulates that every job should be approached with enthusiasm. " If musicians say that they only play ' because the gig came up ', they were not as interested in music as I was in the first place. Or rather, they started playing music just to make money, some people are like that. One thing I admire about Duke is that I think if he lives to be a hundred years old he'd still be in that category of enjoying music. Louis's that way, Sidney Bechet was the same — all the old men. They probably will play until the day they die.

" There are some people who give up and start driving taxis and things, but actually the work has fallen off so much for jazz that I can see the reason for many fellows changing professions. With the decline of the big bands, there's not much inspiration for the young kids coming up unless they play saxophones or guitars. When I was young there were about 270 big bands in the country — every town had three or four — but now you're doing well if you can name ten good ones after you've called Duke, Count and Harry James."

Buck Clayton has little sympathy for musicians who prefer to play safe by sticking to their old repertoire and solo routines. His integrity is such that when he was temporarily indisposed on a recent visit to Europe, he refused to rest on his laurels. " There were many times that I would debate with myself behind stage whether I should attempt one particular passage because it ran from high C up to high G and if you missed any notes in between it would be a catastrophe, a real bring-down. Many people, they're quite content not to bother with those things and they'll just stay in the same old thing, but fortunately, I never missed it. I guess that it must have been thanks to a good horn and a good mouthpiece.

" And this is maybe something that would make me stand out from other players, because I really would go for notes that they wouldn't even think about." Buck likened the lack of adventurousness in some of his contemporaries to the Dixieland idiom. " I don't understand why those musicians play the same thing over and over again. That's just as bad as playing nothing ! If I had to play ' Muskrat Ramble ' over and over, I'd go crazy. If you don't do something new, then you might as well forget it. Anything that's in a rut has no interest."

In the era that nurtured the trumpeter, jazz was first and foremost an entertainment, yet it was through the artistry of men like himself that the music was elevated from this status.

Buck's mind is sufficiently open for him to regard jazz as both art form and entertainment. Musing further on his exceptional musical longevity, he went on : " The roar of the crowd is always beneficial to the artist and naturally I like it, but it takes more than that when you have to practise your instrument three or four times a day. But if you don't get that acclaim, there's going to be a great disappointment. You don't practise for nothing, you have a certain aim.

" Self-satisfaction means quite a bit in jazz, or rather, it does to me. When I'm playing music I'm not thinking about what other people have done, that's the last thing I want to fill my mind with, I'm thinking about ' me '."

When jazzmen reach Buck's age, they frequently begin to panic. They wonder whether to quit the business or whether they can maintain their skills if they stay, and for a man who has devoted his life to the nightworld of music there is often no alternative but to stay. Few men of his generation have other interests outside music, other trades or business inclinations, and even fewer have put any money by, yet the spectre of old age holds no fears for the trumpeter. He is already laying the foundations of a career in real estate that he intends to pursue when he hangs up his horn. He will probably retire soon, but one thing is certain — he'll never give up music altogether, for he loves it too much.

" Sometimes you wonder why certain thoughts come to your mind when you're playing. Say, for example, you're playing a chorus — there's no way in the world where you can say why you play this same chorus different to any other fellow. This other fellow may be younger than you or he may be older, but creative ability, I think, is something that is God-blessed on certain people. That's the only reason I can think of, and that's the reason I'll be around."

Chapter Twelve

Maggie's back in town

I used to go all out to excite people, but I believe that
pretty music is just as important. . . . Music
without beauty ain't sayin' too much.

HOWARD MCGHEE

Maggie's back in town

The news that yet another jazz musician has been " busted " for offences involving narcotics is generally lapped up unchallenged by the public who, for the most part, consider drugs to be concomitant with the jazz life. On the other hand, whenever a musician who has never flirted with cocaine or opium derivatives sees the blaring, derogatory " Jazzman held in dope raid " headlines, it sends a shudder down his spine.

" What people don't realise is that there are not as many musicians as there are coal miners or steel workers, but when a musician gets into trouble, it's played up," drummer Jo Jones has said with especial reference to the narcotics situation. His line of thought is usually pursued by the majority of musicians who are anxious to dissociate themselves from the stigma of addiction, yet the fact remains that the number of musicians who use or have used " hard " drugs is far from small, and heroin, the nemesis of so many jazzmen whose shortened careers are self-explanatory, had a destructive effect on the entire bop era.

Howard McGhee, an earthy native of Tulsa, Oklahoma, was an addict for eight years. " When people come out to enjoy themselves, the pushers and the dealers come out, too. They say, ' Let's you and me have a taste — you can pay me when you get paid for the gig ', and this is where it starts. They figure that if they can turn you on to liking what they have, you're going to go for it sooner or later."

Howard, whose impulsive, peppery trumpet style took him to the top in California in the days when his major influence, Dizzy Gillespie, was the undisputed King on the East Coast, has been " back in town " since 1959. He held sway at a time when narcotics were so common in jazz that in the men's room at Birdland, the dealer had his various packages openly laid out on the window ledge, waiting for customers. Such blatant availability was not exactly typical but heroin and cocaine could be bought then as easily as marijuana today, and as the narcotic was cut less than it is now, a habit was easier to acquire. At the end of the war, this was the fashionable way to get high. " When you get up on the bandstand and you look out on the audience and everybody's drinking and having a good time, you say maybe I'd better have me a drink so that I can feel good, too," Howard explained. "You may have been busy all day but you've still got to entertain these people. So you have a little taste. And it's the same with heroin : you go up on the bandstand with it and you're alive."

Prior to the trumpeter's period of decline, he had worked with the big bands led by Andy Kirk, Lionel Hampton, Billy Eckstine and Charlie Barnet, and during the heyday of bop, he became one of the most recorded musicians of the era. He won the *Down Beat* poll in 1949 and made frequent appearances on wax with every major bop figure, including Charlie Parker, Fats Navarro, Tadd Dameron, Wardell Gray and Shadow Wilson, all of whom died directly or indirectly as a result of drug addiction. As far back as 1948 when he shared trumpet chores with Navarro on the famous Milt Jackson session that produced " Double Talk ", the warning lights were flashing. Howard was no stranger to the self-destructive process. " We made 1,200 dollars each and by the end of the day Fats didn't have ten cents left," he recalled. " He kept asking me for money and I just couldn't believe it. It really was pitiful to see such a talent go. He had a big cancerous sore on his shoulder and everytime he got high, he'd go to sleep and scratch it. It was a tragedy."

Howard's own life story is deeply etched in every line of his rugged, lived-in face. It takes less than a glance at his craggy features to tell just how hard he has lived, but by his essentially good-humoured approach to life he shows that most of the pain exists in the past. He has a very generous nature and time to spare for everyone, but when he is working, he can switch in an instant from his habit of good-natured kidding to the imperious manner he reserves for sidemen who are wrestling with a tricky arrangement. He has only to shout, " OK, fellers, let's run it down ! " and fix them with his no-nonsense glare for the reluctant notes to fall in place. Both as a hard-swinging though mellifluous trumpeter and as the organising genius behind a burgeoning big band of relatively unknown youngsters, " Maggie " is one of New York's most popular jazz people. He is very adept at " taking care of business " in the musical sense, and commands respect at all levels. But it wasn't always that way.

" The way it started was like this. I was living on Forty-fifth Street and people in the neighbourhood started to come by and say like, ' Hi, Maggie, how d'you feel? Is everything cool? ' This was around 1950, '51, and I started hanging out with these guys who'd say, ' Let's get high, let's take a sniff of this or a stick of that ', and so I started sniffing. I thought it was just the thing to do because everybody else was doing it. And why not? I went four, five days hanging out with these guys but I didn't realise until the fifth day that the monkey was on my back."

As Howard himself admits, and frequently, if anyone knew better, he did. In 1946–47 he had worked in California with Charlie Parker, who had been a heroin addict since his mid-teens. He had plentiful opportunity to observe long-term suicide at first hand. "He used to tell me, ' Maggie, don't you ever do this.' But we had been drinking all the time and Charlie used to take a handful of benzedrine and drink a quart of scotch, smoke anything he wanted to smoke and be high but OK. I said what the hell, because it was just a kick to me. But it was a shame that I ever got into it because I missed a lot of the good things in life that I should have had. Bird hipped me but I wasn't too wise."

There are few musicians of the Parker–McGhee generation who did not succumb to the fashionable urge to " get high " in the most damaging way and the death-roll of those who never reached musical maturity let alone middle age is filled with illustrious names. Possibly because their music was created around the end of World War II when the whole frenzied atmosphere was charged with the idea of " living for kicks " and enjoyment at any price, or possibly because of the frustration engendered by the public's delay in embracing the music — whatever the reasons, the names and numbers of those who drifted after auspicious beginnings are common knowledge in jazz circles. Nevertheless, there are several exceptionally strong-willed men who are still prominent on their instruments because they were able to tear themselves brutally from the narcotic cul-de-sac. Howard McGhee is one of them.

Because of the frantic new music's relatively unintelligible nature as far as the existing jazz audience was concerned, those who did appreciate its importance were often thrown together with the actual participants in an awkward relationship based on mutual sympathy. "The era that we came up in," Howard explained, "with Dizzy and Miles and all those cats, everybody was trying to be tight with us because they liked us and dug what we were doing. They said like, 'Maggie's my friend', but the cat might not even realise that he was more of an enemy by turning me on. Nowadays I know, because I'm a little different than I was then, but the average cat figures that he's doing you a favour by making stuff available. Every day he's there and you just get deeper and deeper until pretty soon he's gone and *you're* asking where *he's* at. They leave you out there on a limb."

The trumpeter's initial experiences were confined to marijuana and cocaine. Using heroin intravenously was still a closed shop to him as he recalled : " Miles used to come by the house every day and get blind. One time I went and caught him in the bathroom and he was lying there *out*, with the needle sticking in his arm. That was another problem and I didn't even know anything about it then. All I knew was that my wife used to get mad because every time he came by he'd want to use the bathroom."

Opposite McGhee's Forty-fifth Street apartment lived a " connection " who would visit him every morning to " turn him on ". He still did not realise the extent of his dependence on narcotics until 1952 when he made a trip overseas with bassist Oscar Pettiford. " In Japan and Korea I found that you could get enough of that jive for five dollars to keep you high for days. All I had to do was to wake up and take a little snort and that monkey'd be gone. This is when I knew I was really an addict."

Flying from Tokyo to Okinawa, the trumpeter was suddenly taken ill after a bare half-hour in the air. " Rudy

Williams, the tenor player, said, ' Hey, what's the matter with you? ' I said, ' Man, I'm sick ', and he told me to take a snort. I hadn't got the stuff to snort so I went to the men's room and went into convulsions. I was shitting and puking, eyes running and everything, but when I came back he gave me some stuff and it was OK. We went from Japan to the Philippines, and as soon as I hit Manila I had to go downtown to try to get something because, like, I needed it. And I found what I was looking for pretty soon because all you gotta do is look at the guy's eyes and you can tell what's happening. If you get those pinpoints, you say yeah, he's with me."

Until his shattering experience in the aircraft, Howard still thought that he could take or leave narcotics. " I thought it was simple," he smiled. " Everyone does, but I was real strung-out." When he returned to New York, the trumpeter started making daily trips uptown to Harlem where most of the " connections " can be found. His chronicle of addiction speaks for itself in terms of the limited hours that this way of living left for making music or even thinking straight. It's not surprising that the jazz historians refer to this period of his life as " musically inactive ". " I'd jump on the train and go right up to 125th Street to see who's doing what. I'd get me a five-dollar bag, a ten-dollar bag, twenty, a hundred — any kind I could afford. I was shooting by that time because sniffing wasn't doing nothing for me. I was home but that was the start of the scuffling years.

" The only thing with drugs is that however much you use, every day entitles you to need more. Say you take a drink of gin today, tomorrow you need two, and it's the same with heroin. Pretty soon you can't get enough, I don't care however much you use. You shoot as many times a day as you feel like it, whenever you need it. You say, ' Hey, baby, I think I'm getting down. I'd better shoot up again ', and — bang ! "

The money involved in supporting a habit of Howard's dimensions can be formidable and often, he admitted, " the only way to score is to cheat or steal. You get your money any kind of way." What little there was of his music when he was sick suffered, too, and for eight years every day was one continual struggle to keep body and soul together. Music, until then his *raison d'être*, took a very poor second place. " I worked when I could get to the gig and I could only make it if I'd had a dose," said the trumpeter bluntly. " At one time I had a gig in Philadelphia for 600 dollars and the man had sent me 300 dollars on my salary before I even got there. I got to the gig about midnight because me and my girl had been shooting dope all day. The dope man said, ' I'll be at your house at ten ', and I can't leave until I get the stuff because I've got to have it to play my gig. I can't go up on the bandstand with my eyes running and puke all over the audience. So when I get to the gig the cat is mad and I tell him my car broke down. The next night I was on time and the following one I wasn't even there."

During this particular engagement, Howard arranged for half of a 1,000-dollar salary to be wired to him from Pittsburg where he was to work the following week. " I was still working in Philly but I was in New York every day. When the gig closed I didn't even have transportation so I had to wire the cat again to send me another yard [100 dollars]. As soon as I got there I found that a five-dollar bag is fifteen there and so the week I was there I drew 300 dollars to keep up with that price. The cat told me, ' Baby, you've only got a yard left ! ' and when I got to the airport the last night I didn't even have cab fare. I took a cab to the job anyway because I was an hour late, and I told the man to take care of the cab driver. I was shooting seventy-five dollars a day."

At the end of the last night of his Pittsburg job, Howard had borrowed money from nearly every club employee. He collected his remaining seventy-five dollars and looked around for an easy way out. " I also had pawned my horn before I went to Pittsburg, and a friend of mine that used to play with me in Billy Eckstine's band had loaned me his horn to play the gig. I said I'd pay him for using the horn but when the time came I just said ' Thank you ' because I didn't have a quarter." The trumpeter permitted himself a sardonic laugh.

He took the club's rear exit and then, with the kind of luck that belongs more to fiction than reality, ran straight into a policeman. " I said, ' Baby, I got to get to New York and I ain't got no money ', and would you believe, this cat took me to a hotel and bought me a room there! He don't know that I've got a five-dollar bag in my pocket and as soon as he quit, I went straight on up and shoot that bag. I figure I got about four hours before that shit starts hitting me again, so I start thinking how I can get to New York.

"There's an organ player I know who's leaving for Washington, D.C., in the morning. I know a lot of guys there so I figure that if I can get to Washington, I can get back to New York. We arrive around 1.30 and I look in the telephone book and call this pianist, John Malachi, and I say, 'Baby, I need some money.' And I don't even know anyone there to cop from! I go by John's house and he lays some bread on me but he don't want me to leave. I'm ready to split so I tell him I'll be at his gig that night. I go there after I've copped but I'm feeling bad because a bag there is cut a hundred times more than it's cut in New York. So then I see that I know the bass player and the drummer and I say, 'Oh, yeah?' I borrowed from everybody."

Lies, deception, cheating and stealing; that was the life that the poll-winning trumpeter's habit forced him to live. But the man inside Howard McGhee was stronger than many, and after eight years of miserable scuffling he took a long, hard, objective look at the remains of one of the key men of bebop times. "I got up one morning and I looked like a bowl of kraut!" he reported wryly. "So I said I'm gonna quit because I didn't have a razor, a clock or a window. I said if this is the way the process goes, this I don't need."

Howard paid tribute to a guitarist friend, Jimmy Lewis, for helping him to carry through his decision. "He said, 'Maggie, you look like two cents. Come on out to my house, baby, and let's try to cool it.' And he took me to his house and went and got some pills to make me sleep. I slept for four days and on the fourth day a cat came over and asked me to write him out a lead-sheet. He gave me seven dollars and when I got the money I went straight uptown to cop me a three-dollar bag because I figured I needed it. As soon as I turned the corner, the cop grabbed me."

He was sent to jail for possession although, ironically, he had managed to kick through withdrawal and had no need for the heroin he was carrying. After a spell in the Tombs, the notorious New York jailhouse, he ended up spending four months in the Rikers Island prison where he was put in charge of the band and was responsible for writing arrangements and teaching aspiring trumpeters and tenor saxophonists. " When I found out that I wasn't strung-out any more, I really figured where I was at," he said. " I spent from sixty to a hundred dollars a day just to feel halfway decent, and I wasn't getting nothing back."

Out on the street again, though, it was a different story. Howard found that, with the exception of Lewis, no one wanted to help him regain his foothold in music. " After that I started hanging out downtown, but once you're a junkie everybody feels like you've got to prove yourself, you know? A lot of the guys would say, ' You look good, Maggie. Yeah, you put on weight ', but that was all." Because he was adamant that he would never fall back on narcotics again, Howard could not afford to associate with his former addict colleagues. " The first thing people are going to say is, ' Well, Maggie's back on the stuff again ', so I had to turn down a lot of the cats I used to see. It was like, ' How're you doing? 'Bye! ' ''

The first leader to give him a chance was Woody Herman who hired him in 1960, almost two years after his release from prison. He then spent a while with Duke Ellington but ran into trouble when the band played New York. Although while with Herman he had played the city without the then compulsory Cabaret Card which was withheld by the police from performers with a criminal record, Ellington insisted on him having one. When he was refused this essential by the Police Department he was forced to leave the band, and it was not until the Rev. John Gensel, a well-known saviour of luckless jazz musicians, hired a lawyer on his behalf, that Howard regained his permit to work in the world's leading jazz city.

With his Cabaret Card in hand and a solid reputation for integrity and, above all, being " clean ", the trumpeter has since worked as frequently as any musician of his calibre. But there are some people who will not allow him to forget the past. " I am lucky," he says sincerely and often. " I am so glad that I was able to get off that stuff that I don't know what to do. I don't need it. If a guy talks to me about getting high, I say, ' Looka-here, are you out of your mind? ' But cats that I knew a long time ago, they still come up to me."

He gave the example of a well-known agent who invited him to his house and tried to turn him on again. " I said no, I didn't have any eyes. 'Come on,' he said, ' me and you. We've been out on the road a long piece together ', but I still didn't want to know. And then he didn't hang out with me any more. They found him eventually, sitting in his room. He'd been dead two or three days. Someone gave him a ' hot shot ', they say. That's like, if a cat got a whole lot of money from you or something, he'll scrape off that stuff that accumulates around the top of a car battery, package it up and give it to you. It looks just like heroin. They could have found me the same way many times, many places. At least I'm thankful that I had the chance to come back here and try to do something for somebody else, because a lot of people out here need help."

Through his own example, Howard has helped several men who have been tempted by the false sense of excitement narcotics induce. That he can look back at his muddled life with something approaching a jocular attitude speaks well of his own capacity for readjustment and for the steadying influence of Sandy, his exceptionally level-headed wife. But, as he pointed out, not everyone accepts that his way of life has altered. " I'm through with it now, but a lot of people won't believe that. They don't think that a drug addict can ever clean up, but I tell you straight, I ain't got *no* eyes."

Musicians, by the very extrovert nature of jazz, are an erratic breed. They drift from one kick to another in search of the elusive something that will help them slow down when their minds are clouded by the urge to be different, by the struggle to earn a decent living and by the music's own explosiveness. Small wonder that so many lives have ended in the human scrapyard.

Howard needs none of the stimulants that corroded his early years with despair; he has his trumpet, his music and his band of enthusiastic young players, and this suffices. He likes to relax with the occasional glass of Beefeater's and play

with his pear-shaped dog, Max; then he turns on the music.
Day in and day out he listens to his favourite sounds, the
pleading of Billie Holiday's long-gone voice, the irrepressible
surge of Charlie Parker's vanished alto. It's almost like a kind
of therapy, for these permanent reminders of the personal
tragedy of two friends are at hand too frequently for Howard
to drift back to the clutches of misery.

The trumpeter is an exceedingly warm-hearted man,
although he claims that the warmth is something that has
developed with his increasing wisdom, just as his approach to
the music has altered. " I used to go all out to excite people,
but I believe that pretty music is just as important. My future
plans are to play prettier than ever. Anyhow, I think that
music without beauty ain't sayin' too much." When Maggie
came back, he came to stay.

Chapter Thirteen

The Boss of the blues

Blues I did mainly for the fun of it.

JOE TURNER

The Boss of the blues

It's rare to be able to dub any performer "the greatest" without fear of reprisal, but there are few contenders for the title of World's Greatest Blues Shouter. Even with men like Jimmy Rushing and Jimmy Witherspoon in the running, there is an authority to Joe Turner's brand of shouting that defies comparison.

In spite of his generally accepted status as Boss of the Blues, Turner sees himself more as a rock-and-roll performer than as the man who sang with Bennie Moten, George Lee, Andy Kirk and Count Basie in the prewar heyday of Kansas City. In conversation, he continually recalls the mid-1950s when he emerged from semi-obscurity to figure in the popular record charts with such epics as "Shake, Rattle and Roll" and "Chains Of Love", but although he associates himself with that era, it is not with nostalgia. Characteristically, he regards his short-lived success alongside the Bill Haleys, Elvis Presleys and Fats Dominos cheerfully and somewhat philosophically :

"I made all those things before Haley and the others, but suddenly all the cats started jumping up, and I guess I kinda got knocked down in the traffic."

More than six feet tall and heavily built, Turner views the world from behind lazily drooping eyelids. He is not the kind of person you interview; he's a man you sit down and drink with. He's likely to laugh rowdily into the tape recorder or brush aside the notebook with a well-intentioned whisky bottle. You gather Turner's comments at random, but they're usually quite succinct and amusing, so it is easy to remember them. The story of the blues takes on yet another dimension in Turner's rambling, poetry-like speech.

He was born in Kansas City, Mo., "around 1911". His earliest musical recollections were of street groups. "A bunch of us used to get together in school, too, and go sing in the park. It was, you know, a little quartet, and we used to have

a lot of fun. I never did play any instrument though I did try
to play drums but it didn't work out too good. Of course, then
I had no idea of going into the business professionally.

" My brother-in-law's brother was a piano player called
Charlie Fisher. He used to play a whole lot of piano. Every
time he got a new tune, he used to come home and start bang-
ing on the piano, and we were all excited. As soon as we learnt
the words, we'd sing and have a ball. Mostly I used to go sing
songs like ' Jada ' — hit songs, y'know. My mother used to
take me to church all the time, but I didn't really think it was
the proper thing to do — to sing in the church. But one time
I was in there with this little girl, and while all the people
were busy, we slipped on over to the piano and started wailin'.
So they said, ' What the hell is goin' on over there? Get those
children offa those pianos and things — they's goin' to the
devil right away ! ' And I never did sing in the church after
that."

Schooling and Joe Turner did not go amicably hand in
hand, and to this day he can barely write his name. Music
was always more in his line, and as a teenager he could often
be found listening to the strains of music that filtered through
the doors and walls of the Kansas City nightclubs. It was by
regularly frequenting the doorway of the Sunset Club that his
long association with the pianist Pete Johnson began. Johnson
was his idol and worked regularly at the Independence Avenue
club. Though Turner was too young to enter a liquor-selling
establishment, he had the courage and cunning born only of
youth.

"Finally I got the big idea. . . . I grew a moustache and
everything and put on some of my brother-in-law's trousers,"
he said. " I was a little-bitty fellow then, so small I looked like
the wind could blow me away. I got by the door, slipped past
the people and made my way over to the piano. Pete Johnson
was playing, and I stood around by the piano and asked, ' Let
me sing with your band? ' Well, he just laughed at me and
said, ' Can you sing? '

" I said, ' Yeah, I can sing a little bit.' He said, ' We ain't
got time for no little-bit singing.' So I said, ' You play what
you wanna play, and whatever you play I'll sing.' ' Well,' he

said, ' right now we're playing the blues. You ever heard the blues? ' ' Yeah, I hear 'em every day.' So he asked, ' What key do you wanna hear? ' and I said, ' I don't know about no key — just let me feel around and see what's happening.' And that was it."

Johnson must have been playing in the key of C, for Turner has stuck religiously to that key for most of his material ever since, often to the displeasure of his accompanying musicians. Nevertheless, he protests : " That's an easy key to sing in. Most piano players can play in that key with me, and if I get out of that range, some of them don't seem to enjoy it that much. Once I had some arrangements made in A-natural, which is a very hard key to sing in. To me it was easy. Now when those boys got the arrangements, they said, ' A-natural — what is this? ' So I said, ' Don't bother — just leave it alone and blow from your tops.' There's a lot of time wasted and a lot of energy carrying that stuff [arrangements] around."

Turner eventually landed a job as a bartender at the Sunset, but he appears to have spent more time singing than mixing drinks. " After that, I kept on going, kept right on, and I'm still at it now," he said. " I guess I was around nineteen when I started going all over with Pete's band, playing dances and breakfast parties. It was a six-piece band. I used to get a chance to sing with Bennie Moten when they'd come to town. I'd run up there and tell 'em that I'd like to sing two songs if they wanted me. And then I used to sing with Ben Webster, Jo Jones and all the cats out of Basie's band. We had jam sessions every Friday night. I wasn't making much money, but look at the fun I was having ! Now all the fellows have scattered out, everybody went their own way."

When it comes to his own favourite singers, Turner names Witherspoon, Wynonie Harris, Roy Brown and T-Bone Walker. And he speaks fondly of one of his great contemporaries from the Kansas City days : " For a while Jimmie Rushing and I had it kind of sewed up. There wasn't too many cats come jumping on the floor in those days. If any new cat came to town and wanted to work out real good, we'd say, ' Let's go over there and see what he can do.' And we'd run over to the joint and see him pulling all the things out of the trick bag. We'd listen to him do a number and see if we could make him a member of the club."

But even in the 1930s a good big-band blues shouter was hard to find in Kansas City or anywhere else for that matter. "There weren't a *gang* of blues singers, you know, with the bands," Turner remarked. " Walter Brown was one. Jay Mc-Shann used to come up on the circuit to Kansas City, and that Walter Brown was always trying to shoot me down a little bit," he recalled without animosity. " He had just started and he was giving me a hard time. But it seemed like I'd always come out a little bit ahead of him. Every time we'd get to one of those jam sessions, I'd do him in !

" I was only interested in music then — I ate and slept that stuff. I'd be sitting on the side of the bed till late at night, thinking up some blues. And every time some new blues records came into town, the man would call me up, and I'd be right down at the store."

Lethargic but good-natured offstage, Turner is continually impressive on the stand in his capacity for verbal inventiveness within the limitations of the twelve-bar blues format. At his age he still has the will and the energy to move from club to club throughout the course of the night, doing a set there, sitting in here, and he never appears to tire. Like so many of the men from Kansas City, he worked into this system in the days when every night held promise of a jam session.

" You didn't have microphones or nothing in those days," he said, " and you got so that you could sing and fill one of them big dancehalls with one of them little paper horns. And that was something to do then, even if you could get the hang of it — singing to all those hundreds of people.

" I used to have a powerful voice before the mikes came in. But they was really a fascinating thing. I figured it would give me a nice little riff and save me a while so's I could last out longer. But then I found out that it really made me sing harder. I'd get to singing and it'd sound so good that I'd just keep on. I'd sing three, four hours and never sing the same verse. I'd keep all those things in my head, and they didn't know how I'd do it. But all the time I'd be writing that stuff as I go along. Once I get started into a good blues song, I could carry on for hours.. And I'd get the people all stirred up, just like a preacher. Stir 'em up ! "

Turner's musically rewarding association with Pete Johnson lasted for more than ten years. Some of the pianist's best-known compositions, things like " Roll 'Em, Pete " and " Wee Baby Blues," which have since become blues standards, were written in collaboration with the singer. " Roll 'em, Pete ! " was, of course, Turner's favourite exhortation from behind the bar.

In the early 'thirties when Johnson and Turner were working at the Sunset and making an occasional radio broadcast, they were heard by talent scout John Hammond. In 1936 he invited them to New York, but work was scarce there and so they returned to Kansas City. In 1938 Hammond repeated the invitation, this time to take part in his famous " Spirituals to Swing " concerts at Carnegie Hall. It was there that Johnson first teamed up with fellow pianists Meade Lux Lewis and Albert Ammons, and shortly afterwards the Boogie Woogie Trio, as it became known, opened a residency at New York's Cafe Society featuring Turner's vocals.

" That was a real bang-up time ! " the singer exclaimed, recalling the trio. " Them cats could make up some noise. Sometimes we used a whole band or a rhythm section if the cats was feeling co-operative, but they didn't really need them. They had their own rhythm going."

While Turner and Johnson were based in New York, they recorded on a number of occasions and achieved considerable success before going their separate ways. But with the rise of bop, Turner's brand of music fell into disfavour, and he drifted into obscurity. His considerable talents lay dormant for years before his fairy godmother, in the dubious guise of rock-and-roll, put him back on the map. With hit singles like " Shake, Rattle and Roll " and " Honey Hush ", Turner captured the teenagers' fancy, and with his Atlantic album, *Boss of the Blues*, which temporarily reunited him with Pete Johnson, he reminded jazz enthusiasts of his omnipotence in the blues field. " I made ' Honey Hush ' down in New Orleans, and that kind of kicked off a different beat there," he said. " It was nothing but the blues with a good jump beat, but it kicked off and the others took me over the top."

And quite a long way over the top, in fact, for Turner has been working steadily since. These days he appears most frequently as a single in nightclubs, but on occasion he cheerfully faces up to a round of one-nighters. The struggle for top billing on this type of package show merely amuses the veteran bluesman. " I just get out there and do my bit when everyone's hollerin' about who's supposed to be the star of the show," he said with a smile. "Competition — I call it the chopping-block ! "

He has few complaints about the kind of musicians he meets as accompanists nowadays, apart from an extreme dislike of quiet drummers. "I don't like people that're skipping all around on the drum, or people who play too soft," he said. "My favourite drummer was Chick Webb, but back in those days we had a whole lot of good drummers. People looked then like they was way ahead on the drums. They was more fancy, you know? They'd play all up on the walls, everywhere. It would be pretty to look at them. But we still got a few of 'em left."

The singer lives quietly in New Orleans with his second wife and in recent years has visited Europe twice. There he finds a different kind of recognition than he would in the States where he confines himself in the main to teenage audiences, though he was well received at the 1964 Monterey Jazz Festival.

Jimmy Witherspoon, a singer who has idolised Turner from his youth, has succeeded in reaching a wider, more sophisticated public than his major influence, while relying on what is basically the same material. Witherspoon considers that Turner's laziness has been the main factor in retarding his progress in more commercial pastures. " I don't say that he could sing ballads," he once commented, " but I think that Joe could do a lot more than he does if he wanted, if he tried."

But praise neither bothers nor pleases Turner. The blues genre came easily to him although he has probably experienced fewer hard times than the average blues singer. "Blues I did mainly for the fun of it," he said. " I didn't really give much thought to what was behind the songs. Most of the time I pick out the songs where I feel that I can get the most emotion out of the people. I kind of work at the people in the audience, and once I get them on my side, I let 'em have it! "

Chapter Fourteen

The fire this time

Jazz is the symbol of the triumph of the human spirit, not of
its degradation. It is a lily in spite of the swamp.

ARCHIE SHEPP

The fire this time

Jazz, the music of an oppressed minority, has inspired more than its fair share of social commentators, some informed and many misguided, but seldom has the music produced its own. In the defiant saxophonist Archie Shepp, sometime writer, sometime actor, the gap has been filled.

Shepp, whose hoarse and crying tenor saxophone is one of the most intense elements in the jazz avant garde, is the kind of man you might describe as a "professional Black" if you had never met him. He has written freely and frequently on the blackness of jazz and the fight for freedom, yet the kind of term reserved for those artists and sociologists who seem to live off their blackness by forever lecturing the world about it fits uneasily on his manly shoulders. Archie is, in point of fact, one of the most aware and open-minded men to be thrown up by the jazz struggle.

Above all the tenor saxophonist is objective or, as he would say, as objective as an "ex-slave" can be. He has suffered from the misrepresentation of his image when he had no particular desire to even own an "image", and is vehement in his denial that any element of racism lurks in his makeup. "It's difficult for a Negro to be a racist because we have no power," he feinted.

A semantic confusion has arisen in the language of bigotry because many white people fail to think carefully before using the word "racist", he explained. "Racism, discrimination or prejudice imply the right to prescribe your housing, your education, even the way you think. It implies power. I mean, you aren't seriously suggesting that Malcolm X ever kept white children out of Negro schools?" The penetrating gaze spoke for itself.

As musicians' backgrounds go, Archie's was not the most typical. He was born in Fort Lauderdale, Florida, but spent most of his formative years in Philadelphia, a city famous as the cradle of much postwar jazz talent. In Philadelphia, " a fertile place ", he grew up with trumpeter Lee Morgan and worked briefly with him in both rock-and-roll and jazz surroundings. As an amateur clarinettist and saxophonist, Archie was on more than nodding terms with the local jazz fraternity that included musicians like bassist Henry Grimes and pianist Bobby Timmons, but when he made the inevitable move to New York in 1959 he planned to work as playwright or actor. "Because I couldn't get employment in either area, I got back into playing music."

At school Archie read history and later, in college, the works of Marx and he considers that this background was partly responsible for his interest in the sociological implications of jazz, " something I've always felt very close to. In the first place, the first sociological laboratory is your own life — if you're an ex-slave. I've always observed the people around me, I've listened to what they had to say. I've listened to my father talk and I've learned a lot. He was a banjoist, an amateur musician but a good one, and I knew my father totally. He had a lot of ideas and I took those ideas to school with me and aired them.

" So the sum total of my Western formal academic training and my Southern Negro Baptist orientation was a good through view of America. For me, personally, it's impossible to imagine playing music without seeing my entire history associated with it."

Archie maintained that in jazz you have to study the man himself to fathom his music, an attitude that recalled Rex Stewart's unashamed admiration for Louis Armstrong in the 1920s. " During the period when I was a teenager and everybody wanted to play like Sonny Rollins, everybody started to look like Sonny Rollins, their posture and everything." Similarly, it is his opinion that you cannot evaluate a jazz musician without being aware of the factors that have shaped his life. " You have to remember that Bird was a junkie at the age of fifteen," he pointed out. " And this, it seems to me, must have had some relation to the Prendergast régime that existed in Kansas City at that time, a régime that was one of the most notoriously corrupt in the state's history. That is an incidental fact but it must have some bearing on the development of Charlie Parker. For example, had there been no Prendergast régime and suppose it had been a Mormon society — what would have happened to Bird?

" It just seems to me that whites, and very often it is whites, become a little over-anxious when you talk about what shapes a man. Take a man like Stravinsky, a total man. I'm sure he could talk to you about Russian music and Russian history and you wouldn't be offended by that, yet I always get the feeling that whites are a little bit frightened or offended when I start to include my history."

Ever since the academic critics convinced the jazz musician that his music was an art and not merely a popular form of entertainment, a self-conscious cleaning-up process has resulted that has destroyed a good deal of the music's erstwhile vigour and, for want of a better word, funkiness. " Funk " in its original sense means smelly and dirty, but it's the smell of a living people that makes jazz the most vital sound of the century. In many ways the jazz people did not achieve respectability, they had it thrust upon them in a way that had until recently killed some of the music's intrinsic energy. Archie Shepp and his fellow iconoclasts are once more igniting that fire, although conventional opinion disapproves to a degree of the areas, both musical and sociological, in which they are seeking their fuel. Until recently, white liberals and moderate black leaders advocated a process of " integration " in which the Black would forget his origins and try to merge with white culture, and so it is hardly surprising that some musicians preferred to overlook the fact that the ghetto spawned their music. Not Archie Shepp, for he, like many other young present-day Afro-American men and women, is militant in his Black Pride and has sufficient self-respect not to feel the need for deceit.

" The *only* jazz has come out of oppression and drug addiction and so on," he stated with candour, " although there have been individuals who weren't particularly poor : Ellington and Miles Davis, for example. When Miles was impoverished it was rather by choice than necessity, but in spite of his troubles he has consistently made excellent music throughout the years

So I don't feel that the lilies necessarily have to grow in a stinking swamp!

"That's why I always disagreed so violently with the Russians and the Cubans because of their chauvinistic attitude to jazz. It seemed to contradict the whole thing, everything I'd ever read of Marx, the whole dialectical process if you will. Jazz is a symbol of the triumph of the human spirit, not of its degradation. It is a lily in spite of the swamp."

According to Archie, jazz is on the threshold of a "marvellous renaissance" if, and he smiled, "the bandits don't blow up the world!" As a highly respected member of the burgeoning avant garde, it is more than probable that he is one of the men whose attitudes, ideas and conception will play an influential and basic part in the music's future. "Jazz has plenty of life to it, a very definite future," he commented. He enlarged on the reasons behind the aggressive, raging nature of the new sounds.

"It is precisely because of the emerging identity of the Negro that jazz is beginning to take on a unique character. I think this is obvious in Albert Ayler's music, in Cecil Taylor's, in Ornette Coleman's and in my own. Obviously in John Coltrane's music. 'Trane is due a tremendous amount of respect for the things he did, and when he died, only forty-one, we lost a great man. They say, in this country, that a Negro lives six years less than a white man, and I suspect that as regards jazz musicians, it may be a good deal less than that. This is why the new black expression will play a tremendous part in the shaping of the new ethic — if we allow it to. It's because of the 'have-not' psychology, the psychology of death and constantly seeking to avoid it so that in the end you are not suicidal at all and you reaffirm life in every instance, simply because you know what it is to die. I think every slave and ex-slave knows that and I use this as my basis. This is the life-force that has triumphed in us."

It is a common practice in jazz publications that record reviewers award "stars" to an artist's latest offering. Such decisions are purely arbitrary and subjective and do little to evaluate the music for perpetuity. "I mean, did you ever see Rubenstein awarded stars for a performance?" asked Archie cynically. He also mentioned the ignominy of the original artist (himself or Albert Ayler, for example) being compared or contrasted in reviews with another, superior creator (John Coltrane in the same instance), and described this as being a part of the syndrome designed to humiliate the Negro at every turn. " Frankly, it's the constant psychological debasement of the black artist. I don't think we're treated like artists at all. I mean, having worked in some of these dirty joints around the country that they call clubs and," he smiled wryly, " having been damned glad to be there as a matter of fact, it was then that I knew I was a slave."

Such psychological debasements may be an unassailable part of the black jazz artist's existence, but, as the saxophonist admitted, they are not confined to his race. White jazzmen still suffer, albeit to a lesser extent, the penalties of playing " nigger music ". " Jazz is primarily a black music and the great majority of its exponents are Negroes, but except for those few we know so well, most of them are unemployed. There *are* some whites in jazz music who suffer relatively as much as blacks, and I say relatively because they usually earn more than blacks. The wage scale is higher, as any agent will tell you, and I've had agents who've been pretty frank with me."

Archie pointed out that the unemployed white jazz musician can, if he wishes, turn his hand to commercial or symphonic pursuits in order to keep his family off the breadline, " but Negroes are very rarely accorded that ' privilege '. The same prejudices really extend themselves into every walk of the Western experience and I think that the question of colour is the crisis of our times. It's got to be resolved."

Writers, enthusiasts, and even fellow musicians who have not examined the truths that lie behind Archie's outspoken racial militancy, have continually criticised him for constantly reminding them that their music was conceived a bastard in the womb of slavery. But those who do not have to fight the continuous fight against oppression, either because their race has exempted them from prejudice or because they have chosen to play it safe and toe Mr Charlie's line, do nothing to disturb the saxophonist's equilibrium or quench his thirst for knowledge. He is essentially a proud man whose pride stems not from vanity but from an almost awe-inspiring confidence in himself. He has little time to spare to despise the pettiness and ignorance that lie around him.

On the subject of his critics, he confided, " I've grown rather accustomed to it, you know. Not only is it a myth that musicians are inarticulate, it's systematically enforced because there is no journal for me to answer those who say that we couldn't draw flies. We rather have to take it and bear it, though it comes to be a bit of a bitter experience after a while to read people saying a lot of dirty things about you."

Archie shrugged. " There's no voice for you, no journal of jazz opinion. ' Nigger's got no opinion, it's black music '," he mocked. " Most people think we're inarticulate and we certainly don't have the money to sponsor a magazine whereby we could disprove them. I've written occasional things, which has made me more fortunate than some, but there are many times when I have wished that I had something available to me, some way to answer these pundits who throw out things with impunity like, ' Here. take that! ' and I must accept it."

The jazz musician, whether he plays to please himself or his public, must suffer the criticism of a Press that has little, if any, notion of his aims. Therefore, the saxophonist agreed that he is fortunate to have had the occasional chance to hit back at the relatively large body of reactionary criticism that condemns the new music out of hand. Although his feeling for the music's history was intuitive from the start, Archie added that his college education had played more than a small part in his actual ability to follow the course of its lifeblood through the veins of society.

" You have to remember that a great number of critics have degrees and so on but very few musicians do," he explained. " I think that's a fundamental point of departure simply because, well, why? The nature of jazz is so inextricably bound up with enslavement and emancipation. *Why* do so few jazz musicians have baccalaureat degrees and *why* don't they talk politically and sociologically about jazz?

" Obviously you have to have a fair knowledge of things so that people will take you seriously, but I'm sure that if you were to sit down with Monk, just sort of tête-à-tête, he might tell you things that you don't normally read in magazines. He's a very sensitive man and perhaps not given to talking out just like that, because people aren't made to feel so comfortable when they're not apparently articulate. They're not invited to speak out much, but that shouldn't be a bringdown, though, should it? There are a number of painters, for example, who are totally inarticulate, but it doesn't matter whether you use one-syllable words or four-syllable words, if you can get your point across, that's all that matters."

There is, however, another reason why musicians speak out so seldom against their critics and it has nothing to do with whether they experience difficulty in finding the right words. According to Archie: "The lessons of slavery are numerous and they're not all over. They haven't all been erased. Obviously there were people in Mississippi who wanted to vote for years but they never voted and this happened out of fear which has been stamped into them over a period of four hundred years. I think that legacy is still with us, that Negroes very rarely speak honestly with whites. And that's a pattern that has grown out of history."

The saxophonist smiled his penetratingly candid smile. "You know, it must be a schizophrenic world when one moment you're in fetters and the next moment the slave-master's wanting to shake your hand. The adjustment period is still going on and that's the great challenge of our time. I think the burden is on the white man to prove the morality of the entire Judaeo-Christian tradition."

Just as his music is unique in incorporating an obvious awareness of the past with the insistence of " now ", Archie is in no way typical of musicians. He is more representative of a new type of intellectual fermenting in the poverty of New York's multiracial lower east side. He lives in a studied Bohemian way, surrounded by shelves of dusty but well-read books and periodicals, in a second-floor apartment with no doorbell. The only way of announcing your arrival is to yell from the street. The saxophonist's desire for a kind of anonymity commands respect, just as his imperious, potent music does.

To say that Archie Shepp walks tall sounds like a cliché from a bad Western, but his dignity and persuasive analysis of a complete sector of society make this description appropriate. He is, in the words he himself applied to Stravinsky, a total man.